"No one learns about the d
plunged there by nail-scarred
grace is through suffering almost too difficult to relate. If you've found yourself in a time of soul-crushing confusion, desperation, and doubt about the very faith that once seemed so easy and now seems so superficial, this story is for you. I recommend it with my whole heart."

—Elyse Fitzpatrick,
Author and conference speaker

"In a world full of suffering, each of us is desperate for a good word. We need a word of understanding, we need a word of grace, we need a word of forgiveness. In this heartbreaking and hope-filled book, Michelle Bates gives us exactly what we need, more of Jesus."

—Jessica Thompson,
Author and speaker

"Michelle shares a story that we would all do well to wrestle through. She is an able guide, teaching us the ways she had misunderstood Scripture and helping us use it better for ourselves. She leads us through her story of suffering to a deeper understanding of Christ and his Word, one that holds us fast through the gut-wrenching trials that come with life in a fallen world. Her journey from prosperity gospel to the true gospel of Jesus Christ is both painful and beautiful, devastating and life-giving. I hope this book becomes a resource churches and counselors keep at hand for years to come."

—Wendy Alsup,
Author of *Is the Bible Good for Women: Seeking Clarity and Confidence Through a Jesus-Centered Understanding of Scripture,*
Blogger at theologyforwomen.org

"Is this a story of a family's loss and grief? Yes. Is this also a story of hope and faith? Indeed, it is. But it's profoundly more: This book is the testimony of the suffering God of grace who dwells in the darkness with us, holds us in his love, and carries us forward into a life in which he is the ultimate answer to all our questions. We died with him. We live in him. And in his ongoing love, we find our solid anchor. Read this book: Weep, rejoice, and hope, for the God confessed here is the living and life-giving Savior."

—Chad Bird,
Author and speaker

"As I watched Michelle's story unfold, I kept thinking, 'If she has suffered this much and the Gospel is still true for her, then it will still be true for me.' We need stories like this to affirm our faith and to show us a way out of despair. Michelle is honest and raw while remaining hopeful, faith-filled, and grace-centered. This book will be an encouragement to those who are walking a journey of loss similar to Michelle's and a practical help to those who are walking with friends through their suffering."

—Maralee Bradley,
Blogger at A Musing Maralee

"I met Michelle and Mike at the intersection of Suffering Ave. and Sovereign Way. There they found deep grace and comfort beyond the shallows. As fellow strugglers along the way, their journey serves as a testimony of overcoming love and empowering courage. They have truly experienced God's presence and gracious provision in their direst moments of need. Reading *Beyond the Shallow* can strengthen you for your journey."

—Dr. Billy Russell,
Senior Pastor, First Baptist Church, Bolivar, Missouri

Beyond the SHALLOW

HOW *Suffering* LED ME TO THE DEEP END OF *Grace*

Joy,
I pray you are reminded of Jesus's great love for you and his lavished grace.

MICHELLE BATES

Michelle Bates

LUCIDBOOKS

Beyond the Shallow
How Suffering Led Me to the Deep End of Grace

Published by Lucid Books in Houston, TX
www.LucidBooksPublishing.com

ISBN-10: 1-63296-357-4
ISBN-13: 978-1-63296-357-4
eISBN-10: 1-63296-360-4
eISBN-13: 978-1-63296-360-4

Special Sales: Most Lucid Books titles are available in special quantity discounts. Custom imprinting or excerpting can also be done to fit special needs. Contact Lucid Books at Info@LucidBooksPublishing.com.

To my husband, I only want to
walk this road with you. I love you.

Josiah, Tullie, and Ellison, I love you.
I hope that you see that Jesus is enough
for the rest of your days.

Table of Contents

Foreword

We Americans rarely embrace the topic of suffering and grief—possibly because we find it easier to hide from these less desirable aspects of life until they surface later in life. Maybe we avoid the feelings that come with suffering and grief because of the false security the American Dream fed us from a young age: Work hard, play hard, and you get what you deserve. Most of us are not told that life will include suffering, pain, and grief. In the past, suffering was something that people put away, hid, and removed from plain sight of friends and family. Today, some people have no choice but to break down, get raw, and work through devastating experiences head-on.

In this book, my wife takes you through deep parts of her story that knocked the wind out of our lives like falling out of a tree and landing hard on the ground. At times, our family's suffering felt like getting gut-punched by a cowardly bully who was set on stealing our lunch. On the pages of this book, you will find that Michelle is no stranger to suffering and that she continues to experience bouts of grief daily. However, she has found that grace abounds even in the darkest hours and unfathomable pain that comes from losing three of her six children.

In our culture, it's almost impossible to know how to help a suffering person. Sometimes, we try to comfort the sufferer with words that we hope will help, but sometimes these words can be insincere. I believe people want to be helpful, but often what they say is meant to soothe their own discomfort rather than bear another's burden of deep suffering they can't understand. Michelle addresses this knee-jerk tendency we have to respond shallowly in the face of deep suffering, and she shares her insights about how to help those who are in the midst of heart-wrenching, muscle-tensing grief. Pain is pain. Suffering is suffering. We cannot compare our current or past personal experiences to the experience of another who is in the midst of grief. As you turn the page and start reading, you may be surprised to learn that this story is not ultimately about Michelle; instead, this story points to Someone else.

—Mike Bates

Preface

When my husband and I got married nearly 20 years ago, we knew that life wouldn't be all peaches 'n cream, but we didn't think we would ever experience as much suffering as we have.

As I share my family's story, I hope that you will see that Jesus is with and for his people when they are deep in their suffering and grief. My prayer is that you will know that grace is evident in what is hard. I do not have answers to the whys. I have learned to be content in the unanswered questions, and I have learned that grace is evident, even lavished, in our deep suffering and pain.

A friend once said that I didn't believe in cheap grace. It's true. I don't believe in cheap grace. I believe in grace that is freely given but sacrificially bought by a perfect Savior who suffered far more than we ever will while on this earth. The grace that is given to us when we experience great suffering is the same grace that took our Savior to the cross, held him there, and exploded the grave on Resurrection Sunday. If you are going through an intense season of suffering or if you are simply reading to learn more about our story, my prayer is the same: that you will know our Savior more deeply through these words and that you will be reminded of his great love and grace, which have been given to you.

Paul says it beautifully when he is encouraging the people of Ephesus:

> *For this reason I bow my knees before the Father, from whom every family in heaven and on earth is named, that according to the riches of his glory he may grant you to be strengthened with power through his Spirit in your inner being, so that Christ may dwell in your hearts through faith—that you, being rooted and grounded in love,* ***may have strength to comprehend*** *with all the saints what is the breadth and length and height and depth, and* ***to know the love of Christ that surpasses knowledge****, that you may be filled with the fullness of God* (emphasis mine).
>
> —Ephesians 3:14–19

In our suffering, his grace is lavished, and his love is unending. Jesus is with us. He is for us. Jesus is enough. Always. Despite our doubts, fears of the unknown, and anxieties, he is there in the thick of it. He will continually remind us of these truths till we are Home and he says to us, "Well done, good and faithful servant. You kept waking up, and let me sustain you."

Introduction

Evidence of God's Grace

We used to attend a church in Seattle where a well-intentioned pastor would take a few minutes before each sermon to ask the congregation for mini-testimonies. He called them "Evidences of God's Grace." Attendees would shout out positive experiences of what God had done for them that week. They would say things like, "I got a new job!" "Groceries showed up on my doorstep!" or "We just closed on our new house!" These are truly great things, and certainly, were evidences of God's grace; however, pain that folks rarely had the courage to share was still looming in the room. Apparently, the pain associated with the constant struggles of life did not seem like an acceptable shout-out as an evidence of his grace.

One family who sat several rows behind us were living though a different evidence of his grace. We have come to love them over the years. Their third child was born with DiGeorge syndrome, which is a genetic disorder defined by a missing piece of the 22nd chromosome. (To get an idea of this disorder, imagine a zipper that doesn't line up correctly, and there's a tail on the end of the zipper.) The baby spent months in the hospital before they were able to bring him home because he had to have a tracheal tube in his neck to bypass his small upper airway and allow him to breathe. With that, he needed round-the-clock nursing care; in some states, you can't legally have your child at home if they have a trach. Randomly throughout the worship service, we would hear the suction machine turn on for 20 to 30 seconds while the parents suctioned the trach. You could hear the machine's whirring sound even as folks shouted out their evidences of grace for that week.

It was hard for our friends to come to church during that time, and it was hard for us, too. It was hard for them to hear more joyful evidence of God's grace when they were holding evidence of God's grace in the midst of their incredible suffering. Their child was suffering, and they were struggling with their loss of expectations for who they thought their kids would be. They were holding God's grace in their son, and they were sitting in God's grace because they had a Savior and an indescribable hope in him. As I sat a few rows in front of our suffering friends week after week, I began to realize that evidence of God's grace was breath in our lungs and being held by our Savior amid so much pain.

From my own experience, I know it can be challenging to see grace after the death of a healthy child. It's easy to think that somehow God is unkind and unloving during life's trials. But I also know that his goodness, grace, and glory are not dependent on our responses to our suffering. Instead, grace is simply in his nature. He is gracious. He is glorious, and he receives glory. He is more than good because of who he is and what he has done for us.

When we wake up in the morning, we experience God's grace. With each breath, he is lavishing grace upon us. In each moment of doubt, his grace is evident as he reminds us, through his Word or in a text from a friend, of his abundant love, mercy, and atoning death for us. We typically think that we see God's grace most clearly when things are going well—when a new job comes through, the fridge is full of food, or when the mortgage payment comes easily one month. When people were shouting out evidences of God's grace, I understood what they were saying: God's provision of good things is good. But what I've learned through time and experience is that

God's grace is in every situation. God's grace is most prevalent in the midst of unimaginable suffering. However, in the midst of suffering, it is difficult to recognize his grace.

Our life did not start with suffering. Life was good for us—at the beginning. It seemed that nothing could go wrong—that is, until the spring of 2005. Our reality began to change with a stage 4 cancer diagnosis and the quick passing of my mother-in-law. Over the next several years, we experienced prolonged, deep suffering that comes when you try to cope with the birth of a child with special needs, the death of a son born prematurely, a miscarriage, and the accidental death of another son. Even as I sat listening to the shout-outs of the evidence of God's grace each Sunday, I was dealing with unbearable pain and grief. I didn't see how God was good, and I felt that his grace was absent.

I was raised in church and did all the right stuff. I attended Sunday school, youth group, Christian college, and went on multiple mission trips. I married a Christian guy. You name it; I was a poster child of the evangelical church, and I didn't deserve the kind of suffering that invaded our lives—or so I thought. I had followed the rules.

As my suffering intensified, I realized that I wasn't sure whether I believed what I thought I believed—things like whether the God of the universe was good to me or loved me. I didn't know whether he could empathize or understand my suffering. But I did believe he was real. I believed in the basics: God created the earth, and he sent his Son who lived perfectly, died for me, and was raised from the dead on the third day. Believing this, I had a place to start. So, I went back to "Sunday School" at my kitchen table. I relearned what I thought I knew. Through this process, God has lavished grace over my hard heart and cynicism (though I am still a pretty good cynic).

This book is about my time at my kitchen table, attending my own Sunday School after experiencing too much pain, gasping for fresh air, and seeking comfort from the God of the universe. I've learned that, as Christians, we use many Christian tag lines and verses out of context when we try to comfort or console a person in deep grief or great suffering. While our attempts are well-intentioned, they can inadvertently add to the person's suffering.

As Christians, we commonly portray grace as something that comes to us in the form of a paycheck and healthy bodies. By wading into the deep end of suffering, I have learned that God's grace is much more evident in the mire and the dung of life. Amid deep pain and suffering, I found myself at the grace-filled cross where his glory is revealed in the unseen as I struggle with what is transient.

> *So, we do not lose heart. Though our outer self is wasting away, our inner self is being renewed day by day. For this* ***light momentary affliction*** *is preparing for us an eternal weight of glory beyond all comparison, as we look not to the things that are seen but to the things that are unseen. For the things that are seen are transient, but the things that are unseen are eternal* (emphasis mine).
>
> —2 Corinthians 4:16–18

The words *light momentary affliction* are hard and carry a lot of weight. When we are afflicted, it doesn't seem light or momentary; rather, the affliction feels eternal and reaches into every aspect of our being. It's difficult to not focus on what we can "see." It's easy to see evidence of God's presence when our bank account is full. But when our bank accounts are empty and the mortgage is due, God seems to have left the building. It's easy to see God as big and in control when our children are born healthy and screaming, but when they are born with a disability or sick, God seems distant and far off. But what about "the unseen" referenced in this passage? The unseen is where our hope lies and where grace abounds all the more. How each of our individual histories will unfold, we do not know as the future is unseen and unknown to us. When it comes to our faith, if we're honest, the things that we can see, such as the ugliness of the cross, do not always appeal to us. And yet, God was reconciling the whole world to himself on the cross of Jesus Christ where he hung. Many times, it is at these ugly places where we find the truth. The unseen ways of God are at work when our children die or our parents abandon us or, as trite as it may seem, our friends don't respond to our texts quickly enough.

Jesus is enough. He is more than enough. We can say this, now, when life is good. But when life heats up and it hits the fan, do you believe he is enough? Can he be? Yes. He can be enough, but only if we know the truth of who he is.

So, buckle up and grab your tissues. It's going to be a wild ride.

PART I

A SHALLOW UNDERSTANDING OF SUFFERING

Chapter 1
Christian Karma

"Give, and it will be given to you. Good measure, pressed down, shaken together, running over, will be put into your lap. For with the measure you use it will be measured back to you."

—Luke 6:38

Growing up and early in my marriage, I would see people suffer and think, "How did they make a mess of things now? How did they screw that up?" Looking back, I realize that I was not very loving; I was being unkind and boastful. I thought that since I had my act together, I was going to be fine and live a joyous life with very little harm or suffering.

I believed that if I was good, went to church, had the right friends, married the right guy, went to the mission field, started a Bible club, God, in turn, would be good to me. All I had to do was keep to the straight and narrow. If I said no to drugs, sex, and rock 'n roll, I would be on the path to heaven, and I would receive God's blessings in abundance while here on earth. My unspoken motto: Do good; get good. The typical interpretation of Luke 6:38 is "give and it will be given to you." Often pastors will use Luke 6:38 to preach about money, but they also use the same idea in reference to our behavior: "You do well; you will have a joyous life full of blessings." I have heard that mantra more than once. I believed it, so when suffering came crashing through my front door, I was helpless as to what to do.

I had been fed a Christian "karma" of sorts. But in Luke 6:27–42, Jesus is not discussing Christian karma; he is discussing our self-righteousness. He is addressing our need to love one another, both the people we like and our enemies. He is telling us not to judge others but to look at our own hearts. To see the plank in our own eye, before noticing the speck in our neighbor's. Ironically, I needed a lot of work in this department; I am still working on it and will continue to work on it till I die.

I thought I did okay growing up in high school and college. I grew up in Massachusetts. I am a Yankee at heart. Not the baseball team though. Only New England teams for me and in the '80s, that in and of itself was its own type of suffering! I love the Northeast. I love the fall. I love the snow. I love the seasons. I love Dunkin' Donuts. I love the New England accents: medium French vanillah, extrah cream, regulah shugah for me, please. I love the crazy streets and how hard people are but also how true they are to friends and their families. Friendships are hard to make, but when you make one with a New Englander, you have a friend for life. My husband took this girl out of New England, but you can't take New England out of the girl.

Many parts of that New England culture have stuck with me and influence how I navigate people and relationships. I think the most important thing is that I have tried-and-true friends who have stuck it out with me through thick and thin. New Englanders are hearty. When the Pilgrims landed at Plymouth, I'm not sure they knew what they were in for. There was extreme weather and hard land to work, but they were survivors, and it shows in the rich New England culture.

Growing up, my friends and my family were at my church. If I took advice from anyone, it would be from someone in my church before someone at school. My best friends were at church. We hung out together mid-week, did snow trips, and summer camps, and our families were friends. We stuck together. We shared what was on our minds and sometimes got mad with one another, but we found a way to work through our spats and remained lifelong friends.

I was raised in church. My parents were raised in church. Church culture had a huge impact in my life growing up. I learned about what God required of me and how to behave. I also lived in fear of missing the rapture when I was a kid. I can't count the number of times I gave my heart to Jesus, because I was afraid that I'd wake up at home all alone one day and Jesus would have taken the rest of my family and left me here. I was a faithful member of youth group. I started a Bible club in my high school and went on multiple mission trips. I graduated from high school and lived in Mexico City for a year. I went to a college with a huge focus on missions, and I planned to work in the mission field for the rest of my life. I wanted to live for Jesus. I wanted to tell others about him and what he had done in my life. Looking back, I realize how little I knew the Gospel and how many holes I had in my theology simply because I hadn't experienced much of life.

In 1996, I enrolled in a Christian liberal arts college in Georgia from which I would graduate in four years. A Christian college is a place where a bunch of kids get together and think they know more than the next kid. They come in zealous and, a lot of the time, leave even more zealous—ready to take on the world. I started taking theology classes that required me to dig into the Bible. While reading *Systematic Theology* by Wayne Grudem, I started learning the gospel—not just the Bible stories that I had heard in Sunday School, but a powerful, convicting gospel that saves my life and anyone else's who believes from eternal damnation.

When I was home for the summer after my junior year of college, a friend invited me and some other friends to a bonfire for church singles. That's where my relationship with my future husband, Mike, began. Mike's background was the opposite of mine. His parents were divorced, and he had dabbled in drugs. Jesus saved him when he was 18; he had a dramatic conversion experience and became a passionate follower of Jesus. He ended up moving to Massachusetts while I was living in Mexico City after high school.

I was sitting by the bonfire when Mike came over, sat next to me, and asked, "So, how are you and your boyfriend doing?"

"We broke up about two years ago," I responded.

He asked, "So, then what are you doing now?"

"I don't know. Just waiting and seeing what Jesus has in store for me," I replied.

The next morning, Mike called a family friend and told her, "I'm going to marry Michelle," and she responded, "Don't tell her that! We'll see what happens."

Before we started dating, Mike asked me if I could live in Seattle. He said there was a church there he believed God had told him to attend. He planned on getting there as soon as he could. My response was a shrug and a "Sure. Why not?" I was up for an adventure. Before the month was over, Mike and I were inseparable. He drove me back to school in Georgia.

Mike proposed when I was home for my fall break in October 1999, and we were married two weeks after graduation in May 2000. We immediately hopped into a jalopy of a motor home and traveled 12,000 miles around the US and parts of Mexico before moving to Seattle. Little did we know that the apartment we found online was five blocks away from the church where Mike wanted to attend. I think that moving to Seattle is one of the best decisions we ever made in our marriage partly because it meant leaving and cleaving to one another and wanting to get a lot of time together, to know each other. We had had a long distance courtship and engagement, so the idea of living where we only knew one another was a good one. We ended up living in Seattle for 14 years, and I believe that Jesus knew that we would need Seattle, the church, and his people who were there for those 14 years. We developed friendships with people we will love and cherish forever.

The first few years at our new church were a bit of a struggle spiritually. The Bible was being taught in a much more realistic fashion. We went through entire books of the Bible. Slowly. We studied certain books for a year or two. We studied verse by verse, dissecting the text and learning from it. I had learned to enjoy theology in college but studying theology in our new church was eye-opening. We'd talk about things I grew up thinking I knew, but then I'd realize that things I had believed were often based on verses that had been taken out of context. I had to rethink many issues and ideas.

It was good. I had to start tearing down biblical misconceptions of the past. That time of study was preparing me for what our future held. If I had known the weight of what Jesus wanted us to bear, I would have walked away. As it was, I struggled so much with the Law and rules I was supposed to obey to get into heaven, rather than the grace of the gospel that Jesus had freely given to me through his death and resurrection. There was a new and unique tension that I had never faced growing up in church.

By the time our first child, Josiah, was born, we had purchased our first house and started to plant roots in Seattle. We knew we were there for the long term, so we settled into a good groove. By the time we moved into our second house, Josiah was six months old; shortly afterward, we found out that we were pregnant with number two. It was an exciting time. We really felt like Jesus was blessing us.

As I mentioned before, I hadn't suffered much growing up. I had fights with friends and reconciliation, but no loss or real heartache. My parents were and are still married, and my family is close. I honestly thought that nothing bad would happen to me.

I loved Jesus, and he loved me, which meant that he and I were cool, and I'd be protected from any sort of suffering, right? I was doing all the law stuff, so I figured I would get a free pass. After all, I wasn't messing up big-time compared to others. I had good friendships. I went on mission trips. I served Jesus. I was his disciple, and I planned on being his disciple forever, so things should be a breeze, right? Live life, follow his will, and things will fall into place. Easy peasy.

Maybe it was my naïvety. It was most likely my pride. But I had obviously never paid attention to John 16:33, in which Jesus says, *"In the world you will have tribulation. But take heart; I have overcome the world."* Remember in the beginning of the chapter where I talked about the false interpretation of Luke 6:27–42? I took that hook line and sinker. I believed it. I believed in Christian karma: Do good to get good.

My twentysomething self was ignorant about suffering. I would hear things on the news, but it seemed out of my reach. I had no idea what was about to be introduced into our lives. I thought I had it all figured out because I had been good and had done the right things according to my false idea of karma. The circumstances on the horizon and headed our way were anything but good.

Chapter 2

God Won't Give You More Than You Can Handle?

No temptation has overtaken you that is not common to man. God is faithful, and he will not let you be tempted beyond your ability, but with the temptation, he will also provide the way of escape, that you may be able to endure it.

—1 Corinthians 10:13

For some reason, there is a saying commonly preached from church pulpits and taught in Sunday School classrooms. Maybe you've heard it: "God won't give you more than you can handle." That statement is not in the Bible.

When I was 16, I started a Bible club in my public inner-city high school. I had the help of a few friends and the support of my youth leader, parents, a teacher, and a pastor. It was an uphill battle for many reasons. In hindsight, I don't think I would do it again, but this was the '90s, and I was zealous about looking the part of a dedicated Christian girl. Along the way, I encountered several roadblocks to organizing the Bible club, but with each encouragement from my youth leader, I would hear, "God never gives you more than you can handle." I really believed the saying to be true. The task was hard, but I believed that I could handle it because God gave it to me. I carried this mantra into college. Whatever God decided to toss my way, I believed I could handle it.

Dianna and I met my freshman year in college. We became fast friends and decided to room together our sophomore year. We had it all planned out. All summer, we talked about coordinating colors, the wallpaper we would put up, and how we were going to mesh our stuff to look separate, but cool. We had a great first semester. We would stay up late talking about our families, mission trips we wanted to go on, and things that we were learning. By the time Christmas break came around, we were great friends. She lived near Atlanta, and when she drove home, I would catch a ride with her to the airport and take a flight home. One year, my flight didn't leave until the next morning, so I stayed the night at her house, and we spent six hours watching the BBC version of *Pride and Prejudice.* The perfect way to hang out if you ask me.

During our time together, Dianna and I would discuss how her relationship with her mom had been a struggle. I had met her mother once when I went home with Dianna. While her dad was personable, fun, and easy going, her mom was more uptight and controlled. We talked for months about how they could make their relationship better. We discussed their relationship struggles and in hindsight, I believe my advice was lame and ill-informed. Being just 20 years old meant that I did not have much life experience, but I thought I knew a lot.

On March 31, 1998, a friend saw me in the library, stopped me, and said, "You better go find Dianna. She went running toward the Admissions Building, crying. Something is wrong." I went in search of Dianna and found her crying, hysterically. She wouldn't talk to any of her peers in the office where she worked. Everyone asked what was wrong, but she wouldn't answer them. When I got to her, she was kneeling on the floor. I bent down, asked her what was wrong. She said, "My mom is dead. She killed herself. Just an hour ago. She's DEAD!"

We knelt there, in shock. We had no words. I held her, and she wept.

We got back to our room and started packing to get Dianna home to be with her family. A friend, Katie, and I planned to drive Dianna home a couple of hours away. We would stay with her and her family for the next week as they made plans for her mother's service. When we got there, the house was full. Her dad, sister, and other family members were all there.

It was the first time I had been in a house filled with the heaviness of grief, shock, and indescribable pain. It was the house where her mother had taken her own life just hours before. The feeling in the air was eerie, dark, and uncomfortable. I didn't know what to say. There were no magic fix-it words that would change things or bring my friend's parent back. I realized for the first time that having nothing to say in moments of another's grief is uncomfortable, but it is okay to say nothing. People circled around offering well-intentioned words of comfort, but nothing would do. God had given Katie and me the job of helping Dianna through her grief, but I couldn't handle it. I was just a kid.

Other friends from college drove down to be with Dianna and her family. After the funeral home service, we went to the gravesite. I don't remember the minister's words, but for some reason, I remember the emerald green rug in the funeral parlor. I also remember the picture of Dianna's mom that sat next to the casket. Dianna's mom looked lovely; she looked beautiful and happy. I knew that she had struggled with some inner torment, only because Dianna had shared this with me. When I looked at the picture, I couldn't see the torment in her eyes, only happiness.

All week, we had no words for the grief and pain. Death is numbing—especially the first couple days after the death; those days are still murky and fuzzy in my memory. I remember the house full of people, but it was like they didn't have faces, except for Dianna, her sister, brother, and father.

Katie and I drove Dianna's car back to school with some other friends. We fell into the car, exhausted and ready for the two-hour drive back. My mind was mush but full of questions. But the big question was, why? I didn't understand why.

The year before, a childhood friend had taken his life in his bedroom closet. My parents had called to tell me what happened. I had the same questions then, but this time, I had been in the home of the grieving, with no idea of what to do. I wasn't naïve enough to think that grossness didn't exist in the world. But when tragedy hits so close to home, it caused me to wonder why God has us on the earth to begin with. Even after walking with my friend through her grief, I still believed that God wouldn't give me (or my future family) more than we could handle. I thought that whatever came my way would come from God, so I would be able to handle it. If I was right in believing that God wouldn't give me more than I could handle in life, that must have meant he thought I was stronger than the next person. But I wasn't a stronger person.

By the winter of 2005, suffering was knocking on our door, and the only thing that we could do was to enter into it.

When I was about four months pregnant with our daughter Tullie, my husband got a phone call that his mother had gone to the emergency room. She was experiencing stomach pain, which had been bothering her for quite some time; the pain was becoming intolerable, so she was admitted to the hospital. After a biopsy, the doctors found a mass the size of a grapefruit in her abdomen, and it was determined that she had stage 4 ovarian cancer. We were on the East Coast when my husband's mother called and told him the news. A diagnosis of cancer is a shock to anyone and their family, and it was no different for us.

A week later, we arrived back home in Seattle and drove to Montana to visit her. It was a hard visit. She had begun to deteriorate already, making it difficult to stay there. We stayed for the weekend and went home. A short time later, Mike's sister, Sarah, began staying with their mom, and we would receive several updates from her each week.

Mike had a busy season ahead of him. He had a pregnant wife, a sick mother, and a lot of work travel. Many times, Josiah and I would go with him on his trips to be together as a family. One weekend after we returned home from one of Mike's business trips to Salt Lake City, his sister called on Sunday evening to say that we had to get back to Montana. His mom wasn't doing well, she had just been placed in hospice care and had only a few days left. She had received her initial diagnosis at the end of February 2005 and by May when we got the call, she had gone downhill quickly.

I think we all knew she wasn't going to make it when we heard the prognosis, but we all wanted to see one of those amazing healings we read about in the Bible—the kind that happens at the big charismatic mega churches. We believed, that if our faith was big enough and if we prayed hard enough, the vending machine God would give us what we wanted. That way, the people closest to us get healed, and all the glory goes to God. We've all prayed those desperate prayers even if there isn't a life at stake. We bargain: If God does this, we'll do that. We'll be better, act better, and God will be more famous because he answered our prayers.

We hopped in our car and drove all night till we arrived in Montana around 4 o'clock in the morning. Mike's mom was passing away, probably within the week. Some of Mike's extended family was here, some of whom we hadn't seen in a long time. Some were family members I had never met, and Mike hadn't seen them since childhood. It's weird. People come together when a couple gets married, when a baby is born, or when someone dies.

That whole week is shady in my memory, but one event sticks out. We were all in my mother-in-law's bedroom. She had a burst of energy and was up for talking, and she asked if she could touch my belly and maybe feel the baby move. I sat next to her on the bed, laid her hand down on my stomach, and started poking and pushing my belly to wake the baby up. My mother-in-law said, "I think it's a girl. She's going to be beautiful. She's going to be really special." I remember thinking, "Well, I think it's a girl. We'll see if she's right."

My mother-in-law passed away Friday morning, May 13, 2005. Our next trial would begin precisely one month to the day later.

"God doesn't give you more than you can handle," was beginning to fall on deaf ears. It didn't make sense. If we are supposed to be able to handle life's tragedies, how does his "power . . . is made perfect in weakness" (2 Cor. 12:9) make sense? If he proves his power in our weaknesses, then we should not be able to handle anything on our own. We would need to be fully dependent on him for our strength—even the strength to wake up in the morning.

The phrase, "God won't give you more than you can handle," is distorted from 1 Corinthians 10:13, which says:

> *No temptation has overtaken you that is not common to man. God is faithful, and he will not let you be tempted beyond your ability, but with the temptation, he will also provide the way of escape, that you may be able to endure it.*

If we read this verse in context, Paul is talking about idolatry and sin and being tempted and giving in to the desires of our flesh, even our pride. Paul goes on to say God will always help us by providing a way out of temptation; 1 Corinthians 10 is a warning against idolatry. We, humans, are quick to worship something or someone. Paul takes a whole chapter to remind and to warn the Corinthians of what their forefathers did. God gave everything to

Moses and the Israelites, and still, they worshiped other gods. Again, they gave in to the temptations of Baal and were destroyed by the Destroyer (1 Cor. 10:10). Paul is reminding them that they are prideful, *"Therefore let anyone who thinks that he stands take heed lest he fall"* (1 Cor.10:12). We too, can easily give in to temptation and idolatry that will cause a rift between us and our Savior. This is a reminder that each of us has been tempted. Each temptation we face has been faced by our brothers and sisters who came before us. But God is faithful. He always provides an escape out of temptation. Always. He promised it.

However, 1 Corinthians 10 does not discuss the trials of this life. It isn't talking about the pain, suffering, and tribulations of the world. It isn't talking about uncontrollable life events such as parents dying or loved ones left behind after a suicide. It's not about babies being born with disabilities, children dying, recovery from car accidents, or parents who long for children but struggle with infertility. These are things we cannot handle; they are simply too much—way too much for us to handle.

I have come to believe that each circumstance prepares us for future struggling. We don't always see it at the time. In fact, when Dianna's mom died, I still believed that I was going to be okay and live an easy-ish life if I just followed Jesus. But now, I can see how walking with my friend in her grief, no matter how immature I was, was preparing me for the future.

Even now, 22 years later, I am still the first to say that I don't know how to respond to grief when my family, my friends, or I walk through it. I have learned that the feeble attempt of putting words to grief as a fix-all are rarely of any use. Many times, saying nothing is more comforting than throwing out misrepresented Bible verses. Our presence, love, and support while sitting with our friends in grief is an accurate representation of what Jesus did and an example to be followed instead of filling the silence with words.

When Jesus's dear friend, Lazarus died, he wept. He didn't go and throw words around at Mary and Martha. He just wept (John 11:35). When he saw Mary, he wept and grieved with her. They took him to Lazarus's tomb, and he wept again. Everyone saw his pain for the loss of his friend. He didn't say any trite words. He didn't toss out any verses from the prophets and Psalms to try to comfort. He was silent, and he walked in and grieved with the grieving.

Why is it that our culture responds so poorly to grief? I realize that is a rhetorical question. I don't have an answer. I know that I have responded poorly to pain, even as a friend. I usually spend time pitying the one who is grieving and thinking to myself, "Well, if they hadn't done that, they would be just fine." How judgmental of me! Grief isn't always a result of something we did. It isn't always a result of the choices we made. Most of the time, grief and pain simply happen because of the sinful world we live in. That doesn't mean it makes sense; it just means that it is.

But I wonder: Are these experiences God uses to prepare us for The Big One? The Event that should cause us to be pushed over the edge? The Event that should cause us to question God's goodness? The Event that should cause our family to fall apart and for hate and anger to reign rather than the grace of God? Jesus tells us in John 16:33, *"I have said these things to you, that in me you may have peace. In the world you will have tribulation. But take heart; I have overcome the world."* In other words, he assured us that we would have more than we could bear. It's mind-blowing and seems a bit like a gut-punch at the same time. But in the same breath, he comforts us: "I have overcome the world."

When I read those words for the first time, it was as if a weight lifted off my shoulders. I cannot handle life. I cannot do it. But my Savior did, and he does. He is in the mess with us. He is bearing it. That takes the pressure off me handling life because, when I believe I'm handling it, I am thinking too highly of myself as if I can do something to make him proud of the way I am handling life. It's as if you or I could get a closer seat to the throne in heaven if we could be good and handle life. But that isn't the case. He bled, died, and rose for this. He conquered it all. These words give me the freedom to be loved and to love a Savior who died for my life's unbearable circumstances. Only this truth will fill our hearts with peace and comfort in the midst of strife. The death and resurrection of Jesus takes the weight off us being told that we must handle one more thing.

Chapter 3

You Get What You Deserve

Jesus answered, "It was not that this man sinned, or his parents, but that the works of God might be displayed in him."

—John 9:3

On a spring day in June 2005, a kind friend offered to watch Josiah so Mike and I could go on a date. We had a nice quiet evening, and I ate some of the yummiest ribs that evening for dinner. After our time out, we came home and went to bed, expecting to wake up and go to church in the morning. Instead, I woke up in the middle of the night to find out that my water had broken. I was 31 weeks pregnant at the time. We called the doctor and got a friend to come over and watch Josiah, and Mike and I left for the hospital in the middle of the night.

Tullie was born early on Monday morning, June 13, 2005. Thankfully, my doctor was on call the weekend that I went into labor. I had been put on bedrest when I initially arrived on Sunday morning the 12th, but I moved on to active labor very quickly early in the morning on the 13th. Mike had gone home to stay with Josiah that evening when I went into very quick and intense labor. Mike walked in while I was in the final pushes. He barely made it, and I'm thankful he did.

I knew in my gut that Tullie was a girl. We hadn't found out our baby's sex, but I knew. When Mike told me that she was a girl, I punched him in the arm and said, "I knew it!" There was joy and anticipation in the room when she arrived. I felt euphoric. I was so grateful for a quick two and a half hours of labor, but we were safe, and everything had gone well.

The story of Jesus healing the blind man is a popular Sunday School Bible passage. Each of the four gospels records this story, but only the Gospel of John dedicates a whole chapter about what happened before and after the man's healing. When I heard the story in Sunday School, it was usually the version taken from Luke 18:35–43. The blind man heard Jesus was walking by and yelled for him to stop. The blind man was then scolded for making himself look the fool, but he hollered, and Jesus noticed. Jesus asked what he could do for him, and the man said, "I want you to give me my sight." Jesus did as the man requested and said, "*Recover your sight; your faith has made you well*" (Luke 18:42.) The commentary in the Sunday School class usually alluded to the belief that if you have enough faith and plead enough, Jesus will heal you, but you must have as much faith as the blind man. This is a rabbit trail I'm not willing to go down.

In John's account of Jesus healing the blind man (Chapter 9), Jesus doesn't talk about the faith of the man; he talks about the man being born blind for the sake of God's glory. In John, Jesus and his disciples are walking along when they pass a blind man. Jesus doesn't comment on him, but his disciples do. They point the man out and ask Jesus, "*Who sinned, this man or his parents that he was born blind*" (John 9:2)? If I were Jesus, I would've done a double take, embarrassed that my disciples were so rude. But Jesus calmly looks at them and says, "*It was not that this man sinned, or his parents, but that the works of God might be displayed in him*" (John 9:3).

Since I had an early delivery, Tullie was rushed off to the Neonatal Intensive Care Unit (NICU), and we knew there was a chance of a lengthy hospital stay. Mike followed the isolette up to the NICU, and by the time he came back, I was feeling tired, but great. I was grateful for a job well accomplished and was confident that our daughter would be fine.

When Mike entered the room, a nurse was standing in the corner doing paperwork. He came up to the side of my bed, but he was quiet. He asked the nurse to give us a few moments alone. As the nurse walked out, I could tell Mike was shaken up and had been crying. He took my hand and said, "They think that Tullie has Down syndrome."

Those seven words changed my life. I didn't know how to respond. I didn't know what to say. I said something, but it was stupid. Something about how we could get through it. Something about how Josiah would be a good big brother. I was in shock.

Down syndrome is not something we expected for our family. Like most couples, when we find out that we are pregnant, we expect perfect babies with 10 fingers, 10 toes, and 21 chromosomes with no copies. Seems to me that isn't too much to order, but sometimes, that is not what we get.

I met a lady once, who has a daughter with Down syndrome, who told me a story about someone asking a dumb question. She was in an elevator with her daughter, and a man asked if she knew her daughter was going to have Down syndrome. She responded with, "No, and I didn't know that my oldest was going to need braces either!" It was a clever response, but braces aren't on the same playing field as Down syndrome. I understood her point though when a stranger asks you a heavy question like that, they deserve a clever response. I've never been able to come up with comebacks so quickly. They usually come to me in the kitchen while I'm cooking dinner after the incident, so my husband is typically the receiver of my late quips.

Tullie's birth was a surprise. She was delivered early, and her diagnosis was shocking. It rocked our world. It broke us. Any expectations that we had for our children went out of the window or at least for Tullie. When Mike told me the news, I thought to myself, "Crap. Now she's going to live with us forever." She hadn't even been out of the womb for two hours, and I was already feeling that the diagnosis was more burdensome than joyous. The joy of a new life seemed to dissipate when Mike shared the news. My mind went to a thirtysomething adult with Down syndrome who can't speak or do anything but sit on the sofa watching cartoons. We are supposed to raise our children, and they are supposed to leave the house at 18. I immediately thought that we would be taking care of her in our old age, and we would never have an empty nest.

It may sound insensitive, but the purpose of raising children is for them to leave. To help them spread their wings and fly. To leave the coop. To get a job, have a family and children of their own. As parents, we're supposed to experience an empty nest. At that moment, with the unknowns and the shock, my mind went immediately to what I thought I may never experience.

Mike and I visited Tullie in the NICU. She was tiny and beautiful with her slanted eyes, straight line across the palms of her hands and space between her toes. All three pounds and eleven ounces of her. She was breathing on her own and had the most itty bitty diaper strapped to her. We could already tell that she was a fighter—we were just unprepared for it.

The NICU nurse taking care of her began to photocopy information for us and collect it in a folder. She made copies of covers of books and pamphlets that said all the bad things about Down syndrome. Even when we got home, with our own research, the websites listed all the bad health possibilities: heart defects, gastro issues, intestinal tract defects, more susceptible to leukemia, and loss of hearing and eyesight; the long, intimidating list goes on. It's enough to make new parents feel overwhelmed at all the possibilities. That's just it though: They are only *possibilities*. They weren't things that were happening to my daughter at that moment. At that moment, she was breathing on her own, and her heart was healthy. The ultrasound of her gut looked great, too, and she could poop perfectly. I didn't need to concern myself about *possibilities* because we had a perfectly working baby that just happened to have Down syndrome.

Later that afternoon, my doctor came into my room to check on me. After she checked on me, she backed up and said, nervously, "I don't know what you're going to do, but I need to tell you that my cousin has Down syndrome, and I love her. We all love her; she is my favorite person and a constant source of joy. I know this is a surprise. I know you aren't prepared for it, but it will be okay. Whatever you decide." When I shared this conversation with friends, some were offended thinking that I should have been offended that she would assume we would give up our child. But in her position, she couldn't tell me what to do, but she wanted me to know that she was supportive. She didn't offer me the bad about Down syndrome. She didn't give me all the statistics of the possibilities. Instead, she advocated for our daughter in her own way. We already knew that Tullie was our daughter and that we were keeping her. But my doctor also knew that some people get overwhelmed with the task of having a child with Down syndrome and decide to make an adoption plan. We cannot judge a person's choice to create a plan for adoption for their child. We never know people's situations.

On Tullie's second day of life, she was put on oxygen because her levels were getting low. We thought it would be temporary, but the oxygen tank stuck around for three years. That is a story in and of itself for later. She was, however, making typical strides for a preemie.

Whenever a child is born with disabilities, folks around you come out of the woodwork. I was stopped by strangers at church or the grocery store, and I began receiving emails. People would say things like, "I grew up with a family who has a daughter with Down syndrome." "We have a friend who has a son with Down syndrome, and he is the most delightful boy." "I have a friend who has a friend who has a daughter with Down syndrome." Many of the comments were about how wonderful children with Down syndrome are and how it is the best of all the disabilities out there. Somehow, though these words didn't seem encouraging; they didn't seem comforting. We were still facing a lot of unknowns, and I couldn't get all those *possibilities* out of my head.

After Tullie was born, my parents flew out from Massachusetts, and my dad stayed for the summer. He helped us take care of Josiah, so Mike and I could go to the hospital freely and frequently and not worry about Josiah's care. It was incredibly kind and gracious of them to make that sacrifice for us.

We began a new routine around our house as Mike went to work, and my dad helped with Josiah. I got ready and went to the hospital for a few hours every day. We were like buoys bobbing in the ocean until Tullie was able to come home six weeks later. I thought that after she came home, everything would be fine. Sure, I had a lot to learn, but at least we'd all be together. We could get on with our life.

Once home, she did amazingly well even though she was still on oxygen. We had appointments with our doctor a couple of days after she came home and after that, we began to go to Children's Hospital in Seattle for all her pulmonary visits. We hadn't started any form of home therapy for her, such as physical, speech, or occupational therapy because it felt that just keeping up with her medical needs was grueling enough.

The doctors were concerned that Tullie or her brother might catch a virus at church because, let's face it, nurseries are Petri dishes. So, Mike and I took turns going to services in the fall and winter months to keep Tullie healthy. Since there were multiple services at our church, I attended in the morning, and Mike would go at night or vice versa.

One October Sunday in 2005, I went to church in the morning. It had been a particularly long week filled with appointments, and life seemed overwhelming. I had planned to sit in the back of the church, listen to the sermon, and then head home. However, when I walked into the building, I locked eyes with my friend, Tami, who greeted me. "Hey! How are you?" I looked at her and started to cry. Truly. She responded, "Okay. Let's go upstairs." Tami guided me upstairs to one of the pastor's offices, and I burst into tears. Hard, ugly tears. It seemed that Tullie's early birth, the diagnosis, NICU stay, multiple doctor's appointments, and life were starting to take its toll.

When Tullie was born, I didn't deal with it right away. I figured that God had this, and I just needed to be grateful for what I had been given. I had a child who was alive, and I loved her. I would give my life for her, but Down syndrome was not what I expected. I felt that if I had taken time to grieve my expectations, it would show God that I was ungrateful for what I had. But that was false. I was grateful, but gratefulness didn't make life any easier.

In my conversation with Tami, she said many encouraging words, but one thing stuck out to me. She said, "Sometimes we need to say the things that we keep thinking. We just need to get it out. They may not be nice things. They may not be 'Christian' things. They are human things."

Christians who have grown up in church often have the false idea that we need to keep it all together. At least, that's what I thought. As if we need to walk into church confidently ready to raise our hands to Jesus surrendering everything. When we do, everyone around us knows that despite our pain, we have it all together. We trust Jesus, and all will be okay. In our situation, we had a kid with disabilities. But it was okay. It was all for his glory, and things would be fine.

But when we Christians insist on approaching suffering in this way, we're creating a culture of dishonesty and living a lie when we choose to put up this kind of front; it builds walls that keep us from true community with others. That's what I did. I felt like I had to keep up with appearances that communicated that I love Jesus. That our suffering was just a hiccup; nothing was wrong, and things would be fine. It was God's plan, and we were cool. But putting up that front was isolating because I wasn't being honest about the struggle in my heart.

I was afraid to say what I thought out loud. What I was really thinking was, "I love my daughter, but I don't want Down syndrome. Is it bad that I wondered if she would die so that we would be free of the disability?" But if I really spoke that, it would show I wasn't trusting Jesus, didn't view God as glorious and sovereign, and that I was really thinking, "What did I do to deserve this?"

I was like the disciples in John 9 who asked, "Who sinned?" But at the same time, saying something like, "My daughter was born for God's glory" seemed like a conversation stopper for me. Whenever someone else reinforced the message that our trial was all "for God's glory," I would nod my head in agreement, but inside, the response didn't feel right. Aren't we all created for his glory—whether we have a diagnosis or not? All of the "God's glory" talk started to sound like another common phrase, "This too shall pass. You'll be fine." But the glory of God amidst suffering isn't trite. God's glory is not a brush off encouragement; it's a sacred theological truth.

After Tullie was born, many people told us they were praying that Jesus would heal Tullie of her Down syndrome. If I believe that Jesus is powerful and mighty and is the same Jesus who healed the blind, made the lame walk, and healed the lepers that are proclaimed in the Gospels, then I believe that he can take away my daughter's extra chromosome. Am I and was I expecting this? No. If I also believe that my daughter is fearfully and wonderfully made, I believe he created her in my womb tripling the 21st chromosome. He did that with a purpose and for his glory. Just as he did for the man in the Gospels who was born blind. Just as he did for the rest of us. We were made for his purpose and for his glory.

The man in John 9 had been blind since birth. His parents were shamed and made to feel guilty for their son's lack of sight. He was ridiculed because people believed his parents must have sinned in some way that made their son's life so despicable. At least, that's what the disciples and the Pharisees thought. The chapter goes on to show that Jesus healed the man. But the man's healing caused a three-ring circus of sorts between his parents, the Pharisees, and the onlookers. The whole scene is a bit comical but was intended to put the glory of Jesus on display.

Mike and I did not pray that Jesus would heal Tullie of her Down syndrome. Instead, we prayed she would be quick to learn, smart, and physically strong. We prayed she would be independent and an active part of our family. These prayers have been answered. She is quick to learn, smart, and physically strong. She is also becoming independent. She has chores and takes as much interest in our family as her siblings do. Each day, God's glory is on display in our daughter. His purpose for her as his image bearer and a member of our family is being fulfilled.

Miraculous healings don't always happen. In my adult life, I have seen more instances of death among friends, disabilities in children, and heartache than miraculous healings like those documented in the Gospels and the book of Acts. But just because I haven't experienced miracles doesn't mean that I don't believe that his glory has been on display. No. His glory is evident with each child. With each breath. Whether they've been alive for hours or days. His glory has been evident in the heartache of the surprise diagnosis. It's been evident as our family has learned to readapt to accommodate the beautiful special children he formed. His glory is displayed as we simply wake up each day and put one foot in front of the other. His glory is evident because it is his strength pushing us through the day, not our own. Yes, Tullie was created for God's glory, but so were my other children.

Jesus knew we needed Tullie. He knew we needed her quiet spirit. Her long hugs. Her smile and belly laugh. He knew we needed to learn patience through her slowness getting out of the car. Her siblings needed her love for them despite the times they are mean and unkind.

Tullie has a special sense of knowing someone's emotional needs. She has a quiet, comforting presence. I can recall one time when we had had a particularly hard week. Heavy. It was like a big weighted cloud was lingering around us. It was hard to wake up, get out of bed, and get moving. It was hard to do simple tasks. Tears came easily that week. There aren't any words for it; it just is. On a Saturday morning, I was sitting on Mike's lap. The kids were outside playing. We were holding each other in the quiet—in the heaviness and our grief.

Tullie walked into the room and sat at the table quietly for several minutes. She didn't ask for anything. She wasn't coloring or playing; she just sat there in silence looking at us. Waiting. I looked up after a while and asked if she was waiting to sit with Dad. She responded, "Yes," walked over, and put her arms around us both. Hugged us. Fresh tears came, and we had a sweet moment with our girl. I got up and moved so she could sit with her daddy. She crawled up into Mike's lap, laid her head on his shoulder, and let him hold her.

Jesus knew we needed her quiet presence of comfort. She knows when we need her. The Holy Spirit lets her know, and I genuinely believe she was made for his glory. Like the rest of us.

Chapter 4

For I Know the Plans I Have for You

For I know the plans I have for you, declares the LORD, plans for welfare and not for evil, to give you a future and a hope.

—Jeremiah 29:11

December 2005, I found out I was pregnant with number three. It was a big and welcomed surprise. Part of me thought I'd get a do-over with this pregnancy, go full term, and get a normal baby. At the time, Tullie was only six months old. She had started therapy and was doing well. We were still going back and forth to Seattle Children's Hospital, and oxygen was a regular accessory, but she seemed to be making progress. With each visit, the doctors turned down or tweaked the oxygen. Her heart was still doing well, and it seemed we were beginning to figure out our new normal. God had planned a future and a purpose for us, and I believed it to be one that would be good for us as well.

Jeremiah 29:11 is one of those Christian anthem verses for when times get rough, finances are slim, businesses fail, or when we're anticipating that something good will come to fruition. We Christians often use this verse as a mantra when we want to know God's will for our lives. But I've struggled with this verse for years. Because what I see in real life is not always what I thought God's plan should be for my life. We use Romans 8:28 in a similar fashion: "*And we know that for those who love God all things work together for good, for those who are called according to his purpose.*" We pick out a single verse like these, put them on inspirational greeting cards, and hold onto their promises. But so often, we miss the context of these verses. I held onto these verses assuming God loved me and that his best for me was my happiness, but God's plans don't always line up with our own.

On April 10, 2006, Mike had just returned to work after a week of vacation. Things didn't feel right, so I made a casual phone call to my doctor earlier in the day. I found a friend to watch the kids and picked up Mike from work, and we went to the doctor. We didn't anticipate that anything would be wrong. The doctor saw us quickly, and after a short exam, we found out I was 5 cm dilated, and at 22 weeks along, that sent fear into my heart. The hopes of a do-over came crashing down.

Things sped up from there. I was admitted to the hospital and immediately put on bedrest.

While I was in triage, we met with a perinatologist who told us that our baby would probably die and that if it didn't die, my baby would likely be born small, blind, deaf, and have health problems its entire life. He said that no family would want such a thing, and he suggested we induce labor. That way the baby would die, and it would be better for us and our child because we wouldn't have to deal with the *possibilities.* There's that word again: *possibilities.*

Frankly, we were offended by his approach. Mike felt like going out into the hall and punching him in the face. We didn't know whether our child was going to live or die, but we had no intention of inducing labor that would surely kill our child. The next 24 hours were critical. Everyone thought for sure I would have the baby. They thought that I wouldn't make it through the night. We had friends on call to watch our children, and we were ready for me to go into labor.

But the next morning, we all woke up, and there I was lying in bed with my feet above my head, on my side, and the baby was still in place and moving around happily in my womb. The perinatologist was doing his rounds and stopped by my room. He said, "I didn't think that you would be here this morning. You're proving all of us wrong. Statistically, you were supposed to have this baby last night." My response was, "I'm not the One doing the proving."

I knew I couldn't do anything to keep the baby from coming early. From the moment we found out that I had begun to dilate, we started contacting people to pray for us and our baby. By the end of that first day, Mike was given another week off work, and he and the kids had meals lined up to be delivered by wonderful people in our church. Some friends had invited Mike and the kids to move into their home, so he would be able to get to work, visit me, and not have to worry about the kids.

I was in the hospital for a week, and nothing happened, so I was moved to the antepartum floor and became a permanent resident. However, I was on strict bedrest. I could not leave my bed for anything.

In the middle of the second week, I went into labor. I had begun steroid shots (a "horse bite" as one nurse lovingly called them) the day before in anticipation that the baby would come early. Because I hadn't been given the second steroid shot within 24 hours, I was put on magnesium to stop labor, so I could receive another horse bite.

I had been on bedrest for a week and a half. I was 23 ½ weeks pregnant at the time, and with each day, hope was rising. Maybe we could pull through this. The doctors knew it too, and they were willing to try anything to get one more day. I had gone into labor early on a Thursday morning, and I was put on magnesium for 12 hours and taken off around dinner time. NBC's Thursday night lineup was on, and my doctor wasn't leaving the hospital because she felt certain that I would be going into labor.

The next morning, she walked in and said, "I slept here last night. I didn't go home. I knew that you were going to have this baby. I thought, 'After *Friends,* she'll have the baby.' Then you didn't. Then I thought, 'After *Will & Grace.* After *The Office.* After *ER.*' You didn't have the baby and I slept all night." We had hope again. There was an isolette waiting for my baby, and we didn't have to use it. The baby was staying put. And the baby stayed put for another week and a half. Even after an amnio test to find out whether there was an infection in the fluid, the baby was holding steady.

At this point, my parents came, and we were talking about me going home. If I was going to stay pregnant, I could stay pregnant at home and just go back and forth to the doctor. With my parents once again in town, Mike and the kids moved back home, and my parents hung out with the kids. We thought for sure things were going to work out. That this baby would make it. All signs were leading to the hope that things would be successful.

But on a Sunday evening, I began to have some back pain. I thought it was because I had been sitting in bed for three weeks. The nurses brought a heating pad and it eased. I woke up the next morning, uncomfortable, but okay. My parents brought the kids for a visit, and things began ramping up. I was in labor. Mike was at work.

They rushed me to labor and delivery, and Mike walked in while I was in active labor. My doctor had warned me that it would be fast. I had delivered Tullie in two and a half hours, but this one would come quicker. As labor progressed, my bag of water broke; it was filled with the infection that had caused me to dilate. My doctor could see it and smell a horrible odor.

As I began to push, the placenta detached too quickly from the uterus and made our tiny baby much more slippery. The baby rotated with each push, and it doesn't matter how small a baby is, it can't exit with its shoulder. I was in an incredible amount of pain, and an emergency C-section was urgently needed. My labor had progressed quickly, and I hadn't been given any drugs. As I was taken out of the labor and delivery unit, I heard a nurse ask my doctor, "What are you going to do?" Her response was, "I don't know yet."

Exiting labor and delivery, going to an operating room, putting me under, making the abdominal incision, and pulling the baby from my stomach took two and a half minutes. Eli Preston Bates was born on Monday, April 25, 2006, at 1:13 in the afternoon and weighed in at 1 lb. 13 oz.

My husband couldn't be there for the birth because of the high emergency status of the situation, so he was left standing in the hallway pleading with Jesus for the lives of his wife and his child. Eli and I almost died that day. Our lives were truly in the hands of our Creator—as they are every day.

Eli was whisked to the NICU, and I was put in recovery. Mike was able to see him and spend time with him, and Mike says that I asked a dozen times as I was waking up from the anesthesia what kind of baby we had and if the baby was okay. I met our son later that evening for the first time, groggy from being loaded with serious pain meds.

Mike spent the night and early morning bouncing between our two rooms, praying for us both. Eli was 25 weeks. He was a white baby boy. Both his lungs were collapsed. He had an infection. He was incredibly little. He was also very beaten up due to the difficult labor. He had four tubes in his body for support. His chances were slim. Very slim.

I had been on bedrest for three weeks. My body was weak. I had undergone emergency surgery and had lost an incredible amount of blood. I was beaten up, but I would be okay. The next morning, the NICU doctor came in and said that they did as much as they could, but Eli was going to die. They couldn't save him.

Mike and I went up to the NICU and held our son for the first time and wept over him. As the wires were taken off his body and the tubes taken out, he was passed between us, and our son was taken Home.

Even nearly 13 years later as I type this, I have no words to express my feelings. I feel like I am coming up empty. I remember the day, but it is hazy. The pain was deep, and I was in shock. I had truly thought that my kid had a chance to survive. I felt like I had done all that I had been told to do, so why was he born so early? I thought Jesus loved me. Why didn't he save my son? We prayed. We had armies praying. Aren't people's lives saved when people pray? There are YouTube videos about it, and preachers preach it. I even bargained with God. Didn't bargaining work? Even today. I have questions and no answers. I probably never will.

Mike and I left the hospital the next day. The nurses were surprised. They hadn't seen a C-section patient leave so early, but my doctor knew that I had been there long enough and that I would probably heal better at home anyway. My body was weak, and I had lost a lot of blood. I was going to need a lot of rest in order to get back to life.

When Mike and I got into the car, we drove home for the second time in less than a year without a baby. But this time, our baby was never going to come home. Ever. He was going to go to the funeral home, and we had preparations to make for the service.

As we approached our street, I told Mike that I couldn't go home yet and asked if we could sit at the park. We drove to the park, sat in the car, and watched kids on the playground equipment. It's still shocking to me that life keeps moving when we are in deep grief. Kids still play. People still go to work, pump gas, and pay bills. People laugh, and the sun still shines. The moon will rise, and the world will keep spinning on its axis. And we can be suffocating with grief.

I remember having the same thoughts run through my mind when Dianna's mom died years earlier. We were driving to the cemetery and I thought, "Doesn't anyone else care?" I believe these are the moments when the loneliness of grief sets in. The grief was so heavy; it seemed like everyone around me should've known that my child had died, even if they didn't know me. My world had stopped; everyone else's should too.

Over the next several days, we began working with friends for a service for Eli. Our church had been praying, and a lot of friends had helped take care of needs around our house while we were gone. They delivered meals to Mike and the kids and continued bringing meals during my recovery.

As we were sitting in a friend's house planning Eli's service, 2 Corinthians 4:16–18 came up:

> *So we do not lose heart. Though our outer self is wasting away, our inner self is being renewed day by day. For this light momentary affliction is preparing for us an eternal weight of glory beyond all comparison, as we look not to the things that are seen but to the things that are unseen. For the things that are seen are transient, but the things that are unseen are eternal.*

Those verses pierced me. They were a balm to my soul. They also created a tension I wasn't sure I could live out. The heaviness of the affliction seemed neither "light" nor "momentary."

Our service for Eli consisted of hymns, "It Is Well with My Soul" and "Solid Rock." I wanted hymns and scriptures of hope, even though I wasn't feeling any.

Now that Eli had gone Home, Mike wanted to be busy with his hands. He wanted to make something for his second born son. Along the fence line, lay several pieces of applewood left over from the winter. Mike found a piece in the pile that was solid and perfect enough to carve out an urn. For hours, he worked in the garage, keeping his hands busy creating an urn for our son. He cut. He chiseled. He sanded, and he worked tirelessly on a beautiful urn that sits on top of our piano. No one knows it's an urn unless they look at the inscription on the top. It sits in our house where we can all see it and remember Eli daily.

In time, I began to feel better physically. Most days, I would take a two-hour nap in the afternoon and slowly over time, I began moving around the house. I started to take on more household responsibility and caring for the kids. My mom had stayed and served our family well, but it was time for her to go back to Massachusetts. She had kept our family from sinking over those weeks, feeding and clothing the kids and allowing me to rest while Mike went back to work.

She also had the difficult task of having a grieving daughter and mother on her hands. A few days after Eli's delivery, my milk came in. My body was ready to feed my son. My son wasn't there to be fed. My son had gone Home. Having your milk come in after a child has died is one of the hardest, most grievous things for a mother to push through. My mom helped me bind my breasts to stop producing milk as I wept and missed my son. She picked up the pieces of our dirty, unkempt household. She helped with a busy toddler and our special needs baby who was still on oxygen. She didn't allow her grief for me or her grandson to interfere with the tasks that had to be done. I'm sure when she got home to my dad, she collapsed in exhaustion and cried for us and their own loss of a grandchild.

When Mom went home, things in my household got back to normal as best they could. But the stress was palpable. There was a heaviness in even the normal tasks. Things were hard. I would usually make it through the morning, put the kids down for a nap, and then go take one myself. Grief, pain, sorrow, anger, and frustration were beginning to mount up to a lot of chaos over the next several months. I was beginning to think that God had left me out in the cold.

A couple of months after Eli went Home, I had a dentist appointment. They knew that Eli had gone Home, and when the dentist came in to greet me, he said, "I'm sorry that this happened to you, but you have two other great kids. You should be grateful because some people can't have any." Just like that I got punched in the gut by a dentist.

I know that infertility is a serious heartache. I know that it is hard; people who are unable to have children experience deep grief. However, my dentist negated the fact that I had delivered a child and buried one. I was grateful for my other two children; I had never mentioned that I wasn't. I had also never mocked other people's pain in not being able to have children.

For some reason, our culture puts the length of a child's life on some sort of scale. If a child passed away in utero through a miscarriage or was born still, then that grief can only last so long. But if a family delivered a child, then that grief can last longer. I've heard people say, "Oh, well, he was only a pound. You must be doing a lot better now that that is behind you." But as Dr. Seuss says, "A life is a life no matter how small." The parents and family members grieve even the smallest life.

Our response to those who grieve can be so trite. We try to say things to come across as smart, but usually walk away leaving hurt and pain. So many times, I walked away feeling angry with people who were trying to provide comfort. Their words were lost on me. There was nothing to say.

We had a pile of sympathy cards laying on our kitchen table. Mike came home one day from work, and I told him, "You better read these cards, because I'm throwing them in the trash. This is your opportunity." He started sifting through them reading each one and asked, "Are you sure? Do you really want to throw these away? Just save them. Put them in a box and hold onto them." So, I did, grudgingly.

As Mike was looking through the cards that day, he opened one that said, "No words. Praying." That ended up being our favorite card. It is on the top of the pile, I think, in that box. It's true. There are no words for this kind of pain. There are none. I appreciated that the signer of the card knew that.

Getting back into real life after a tragedy is hard. It's hard to hop back into life with the people you have done life with before. The meals eventually stop. People stop calling to check in. Cards stop coming. And everyone goes back to life, but I was left wondering how to get back to it.

Reflecting on Jeremiah 29:11, I would laugh at the verse when it stood alone. It was almost insulting to me. Really? He knows the plans he has for me? A hope and a future? If this was my hope and future, then this was more than lame. I was a complete wreck, and I didn't believe that this was my future even though I was clearly living it. But Jeremiah wasn't talking about being happy. God's people were exiled from Jerusalem. They were having a rough go of it, and it had been prophesied that they would be exiled. The Israelites were worshipping false gods. The kings had been leading them astray. They were looking to man for glory rather than their Creator. God had had enough.

Jeremiah is called the lamenting prophet. I can get behind a prophet like this. He wept for his people. He cried out to God to save them, and he believed God's words when God said he was going to save them. But God never said, "I'm going to save you from your uncomfortableness so that you will feel good." He said, "I will be with you in this mess." God was going to save them from the hold of the Babylonians, yes, but he intended a much better Rescuer for them. For us.

What is God's plan for us? It isn't to harm us, but rather to give us something wonderful. His plan is to give us his Son. Jesus is our future and our hope. Not the amazing jobs. Not the glorious house. Not the perfect marriage and children. Not perfect health. God's plan for us is to believe. His will for us is to be his children. Should we pray and ask for wisdom in decisions that we need to make? Yes, of course, but when we belong to him, we are in his perfect will. We have a hope and a future in him. Everything else is just life happening.

The truth is, everything else in life is hard. It is really, really hard. We want to believe that this isn't all there is. That this is life in the muck and the pain. For such a long time, I sat in the muck waiting to be rescued, but Jesus is my Rescuer. Your Rescuer. He is in the muck with us. He lived in and through the muck so he can be with us and understand it.

Jeremiah 29:11 is not simply for inspirational greeting cards; these are rich, beautiful words when they are read in the context of the chapter in which they are written. They are not for our earthly happiness but for our eternal joyful purpose in and with our Rescuer at Home.

Chapter 5

Vending Machine God

Delight yourself in the LORD, and he will give you the desires of your heart.

—Psalm 37:4

When I read Psalm 37:4 in college, I thought that I would get what I wanted, and what I wanted was a particular relationship. I thought, "If I just read more of my Bible, Jesus will give me what I want." In hindsight, this thinking seems ridiculous, but is it? Isn't this how this verse is preached? "Delight yourself in the LORD . . . ." Always think about him. Read his Word, and he will give you what you want. And we better be happy while we read the Word, because if we aren't happy, then we aren't delighting.

I guess this may sound a bit cynical, but when I was on bedrest with Eli, I was reading and praying and so were my husband, family, and extended community. My desire was that my son would be okay and live. He wasn't okay, and he didn't live. He went Home far too early.

We take an idea from this verse that our desire is what we want—what our flesh wants. We want happiness, healthy kids, and a peaceful marriage. We want new cars, big houses, and more than we need. We want what we want. We don't want death. We want peace on earth.

In the aftermath of Eli's death, chaos loomed over us, because I wanted my son back, and we were trying to figure out life again. Life without the child we prayed God would let live. But God didn't see that to be fit. It's tough to balance that. The desire of my heart? Rather, it was a rip in my heart that I didn't think would heal.

Eli changed me, but not in the way that Tullie did. For a while after Eli, Mike and I were nervous about the internally dark places I would go and the possibility that I would stay there. The grief process is beyond brutal. It can get so dark and lonely, and it's incredibly easy to spiral down into a depressive hole. It's easy to become cynical, frustrated, unkind, and isolated and to begin building strong walls around yourself. Even the people who live with you get blocked out even though they are grieving just like you are. Isolation is easy. Very easy.

We were two grieving parents who didn't know how to grieve or help one another. Mike threw himself into work. I threw myself into self-pity and was content to be in the depths of despair.

In his book *New Morning Mercies*, Paul Tripp wrote:

> Envy has its roots in the selfishness of sin. Envy is self-focused; because it's self-focused, it's entitled; because it's entitled, it's demanding; because it's demanding; it tends to judge the goodness of God by whether he has delivered what you feel entitled to; and because it judges God on that basis, it leads you to question his goodness. Because you question God's goodness, you won't run to him for help. Envy is a spiritual disaster.[1]

When I read this, I realized that Tripp was describing me. I was envious, and I was partially aware of it. I wanted a "normal" kid, and I wanted my son back from the dead. I would walk into church and feel judged. Feel pitied. Feel scrutinized. I felt like I could hear the thoughts in people's heads when we walked in: "How could that family

[1] Paul David Tripp, *New Morning Mercies: A Daily Gospel Devotional* (Wheaton, IL: Crossway, 2014), Reading for February 22.

be holding up? They've been through so much." "Their life has been so hard." "So much tragedy in their life. What did they do to deserve it?" "They seem so good. Why them?" These were the thoughts that I *thought* people were thinking. I have no idea whether my thoughts were true or not. I had gotten so insecure talking with people.

Every time someone asked how I was, I thought they were digging for dirt to share with a friend. I didn't trust many people. I also thought I had a time limit in which to "get over it." I was waiting for the time to expire, and I wasn't sure when that would happen. I didn't know how much grace I'd be given, but I felt like it wasn't much. I also realize now that I was putting that pressure on myself.

I was envious of each family that walked into the church building. The ones with girls that were born around the time Tullie was born—the ones who were "normal." I was envious of the people who got a positive prenatal screening for Down syndrome, but whose babies were born just fine. Was I supposed to have had that test done? If I had, would our baby have been okay? I realize that is far-reaching, and I can't change God's plan for our family. I was envious of the people who'd walk into church with their babies without oxygen hanging around their necks. I was envious of the babies who were coming up on their first year who were walking, while my daughter was barely sitting up.

Each week, there was something new to be envious about. I would worship Jesus and say I was fine, but in my heart, I was envious. I could not have what others had, and because I was envious, I did not believe in God's goodness towards me. He was only good to all the other people who had their normal kids who would be brought from the nursery to the main sanctuary to sing with the rest of the congregation till the end of the service. I was heading towards spiritual disaster.

We questioned a lot. We would wonder what we had done to deserve such pain and suffering. If I had believed in reincarnation, I would have wondered what my previous self had done. But instead, it seemed enough just to go through my own catalogue of wrongs to figure out the why of our suffering. But I couldn't figure out the why—not here on earth. I knew that, but I felt like I needed a reason. Someone or something to blame. It seemed easier to blame myself for a mistake I had made rather than to live with the unknown, which was full of suffering.

The summer of 2006 after Eli went Home, we had a rental house that we decided to put on the market. In order to avoid paying capital gains, we had to move into the house for two weeks while we worked on the house to get it ready to put on the market. We affectionately call this summer the "Summer from Hell." When we talk about this summer, we'll say, "Remember, it happened during the Summer from Hell?"

Mike threw himself into work and, in his spare time he painted walls, fixed leaky faucets, adjusted floorboards, and removed popcorn from ceilings. I was trying to care for the children and do house projects (which I was horrible at); it was a balancing act I wasn't good at. Friends would ask me how I was doing, and I would say, "Fine." But I wasn't doing fine. Mike and I weren't doing fine.

We fought a lot. I wasn't doing enough, and he wasn't doing enough for me. It was a constant battle, but somehow, we liked each other long enough to get pregnant again. It was July—after Eli had just been born a few months earlier.

In July 2006, we were getting ready to move back into our house, and I was running an errand at Target. For several days, I had been struggling with acid reflux, a sure symptom that I was pregnant. A week before, I had hosted a baby shower for a dear friend and had jokingly said that I hoped I wasn't pregnant. But as I roamed through Target, I had a serious feeling that I might be pregnant. To say that I was terrified would be an understatement. So, I bought a pregnancy test kit just to make sure. Life is funny. It's full of surprises.

We were making trips back and forth from the property to move our personal items back to the house where we were living, hoping to get back to normal life. During one of these trips, I decided to quickly take a pregnancy test even though I was confident it would be negative. The test was positive.

I didn't know whether I should tell Mike right away or wait until we had been settled into our house for a bit. But I also knew Mike and I were straight with each other. All the time. So, I took the bull by the horns and while Mike was bringing something into the house, I blurted out, "I'm pregnant."

"What? What?!?! Yeah!!!!" was my husband's encouraging response. He was excited. I fell into his arms and cried. I was scared and nervous. I knew that beyond a shadow of a doubt, I was not ready for this. I could not handle it.

We called our doctor the next Monday, and we had an ultrasound that day. Sure enough, I was pregnant. Due in April. When I came home that day, I was sitting on the floor playing with Tullie rolling a ball back and forth. She would catch the ball and toss it back. I rolled it back. She was smiling. I was going through the motions. Grinning at the appropriate times. Engaging. Kinda.

Mike was sitting and browsing the computer, and he turned to me, "You wanna go to Texas this weekend? Let's go. Let's go see the Preskenis. Let's leave Thursday." I responded, "Let's leave Tuesday. After that party we must attend, let's just go."

So, we did. We left. We left without telling anyone. Wednesday morning of that week because Tuesday didn't work out. We didn't tell our friends. We didn't tell our family. We got into a motor home, put the kids' car seats in it. Got food. Got bedding. Got clothes and we left. Silently. Hurting. Wanting to be healed.

Mike and I didn't talk much while driving. We were in Wyoming one night at a rest area, and the kids were asleep when Mike broke the ice, "You aren't talking. I'm losing you. You need to talk to me."

Right there at a rest area in Wyoming, I lost it. We had either been fighting or avoiding each other all summer. We were hurting, and I was terrified of having another baby that might have special needs. I was scared that the baby would die. I thought that I was a burden to my husband. I was afraid of everything. So, I let it all out and sobbed.

The thing about grief is we all respond in such different ways. My husband didn't respond to grief the way I wanted him to, and I didn't respond the way I wanted to. We may be married, but we are still two very different people. When we assume what the other is thinking, we put up walls to keep each other out. I pushed everyone away. Either they weren't responding the way I wanted them to, or I didn't want to burden anyone and pretended everything was fine.

We didn't solve all our problems at that rest area, but we broke the ice. It had to get broken. It was getting very thick. We fell asleep in one another's arms that night. We were gone on our trip for six weeks. Mike had been given a medical leave of absence because of everything that had happened in the previous year. We had to recoup. We had a good trip, but we still had to come home. We already knew that this would be a high-risk pregnancy, and I was going to get to hang out with my favorite OB doctor again.

Mike and I went in for an ultrasound at 12 or 13 weeks, and it was a looooooooong ultrasound. We were nearing the end and I had to go to the bathroom. The technician was pushing and tapping hard with the wand on my belly. After a while, I asked, "What are you looking for?"

She said, "I really need the baby to move. I need to measure its neck." I asked, "Why? What's the big deal?" She said, "The measurement of the back of the neck is a marker for Down syndrome. This could totally change your care."

Mike was sitting in the corner looking at a magazine. He looked up and in an unconcerned voice said, "Who cares? We already have one." The technician stopped what she was doing and looked at me and then at Mike. "Really?" Mike and I start laughing. The technician was as embarrassed as a person can get. She started apologizing and mumbling and . . . well, the situation was quite comical. Probably more for Mike and me than for her. She didn't know our situation, because she hadn't taken the time to read my file.

I loved Mike's response. The technician had no idea what to do with the situation. Our reaction showed her that having Tullie wasn't as horrible as she thought it would be. Having a kid with Down syndrome may be difficult, life-altering, world-crushing, and a punch in the gut, but those life experiences change you. They affect your life in real ways, and your life doesn't continue on the same. The nice, cozy world we try to create for ourselves gets turned upside down. It's like emptying a bag of Legos onto the floor. A lot of the time, we keep stepping on those Legos screaming in pain.

My pregnancy with Ellison was stressful. Not just physically stressful, but financially stressful (because we were paying two mortgages) and emotionally stressful for Mike and me. Josiah was three, and Tullie was barely two, so who knows whether they picked up on stuff. We were stretched thin in a lot of areas for months.

As part of our "Keep The Baby In" plan, I went to the doctor every two weeks, got shots once a week, visited perinatology once a month, got a cerclage (they sew up the cervix), didn't lift anything over 10 pounds, couldn't be physically intimate with my husband, and tried to maintain some sort of emotional calm. We did okay with most of this except for the last two on the list. Things were hard and stressful, and we were still a grieving couple coming from a surprise diagnosis and a son who had passed away less than a year before. We didn't have our act together, and we were hurting badly.

Living day to day can get monotonous, and it did for us. Mike would wake up, get me up, get Tullie out of her crib, put her on my lap; I would feed her the morning bottle, slide her off my lap, and she would hang out on the floor until Mike got home from work.

If I had a doctor's appointment, I had a sitter lined up for the kids because I couldn't get them in and out of the car. Life happened on the floor for about seven months. Therapists came in and out of the house to work with Tullie. They would help me put her in a seat if she had to be in one. Josiah walked around and hung out with me and Tullie. Visitors would come occasionally, and we tried to make the best of it.

We were paying two mortgages because our rental house wasn't selling. Money was tight. The stress of the pregnancy, finances, grief, and just trying to make it day to day was more than Mike and I could bear. Mike and I were on edge, and we fought often. We both were on guard, and tempers flared. None of this was the "desire of my heart."

Ellison Reece Bates was born on a Tuesday morning, April 10, 2007, exactly a year after I had been admitted into the hospital with Eli. Ellison's delivery was boring, beautiful, and uneventful. She entered this world screaming. The first words out of my mouth was, "Is she okay?" Everyone in the room assured me that she was perfect, and she was.

We had been through so much. We'd had a baby born with disabilities. I'd delivered a baby that had died. But Ellison had come full term. She had no physical features of a disability, and she was born with a fighting spirit. She was ready to tell the world that she was here, and she did.

After everything that we had done to "keep the baby in" was complete, all the medical concerns faded away. The baby was out and healthy. A peace and relief had come over us. We hoped a form of healing after several years of suffering could come upon our household.

It wasn't until a few years later that I even understood Psalm 37:4. My desires are human desires. I look at the transient. I look at what fades away and turns to dust as my hope, my truth. I don't naturally look eternally. It's not in my nature, and it's not in yours either. We want what our heart wants—stuff and people to fill the void of those desires that only Jesus truly can.

When we delight ourselves in the Lord, we want more Jesus, which is the desire of our heart.

When I read this verse while I was on bedrest with Eli and during my grief and cynicism, I thought, "He gives me my desires when I seek him, so why don't I have any of my desires (my children healthy and alive) fulfilled?" My heart was misplaced. I was looking at the transient. I wanted my pain to be relieved, but I wasn't going to get that; rather, I was going to learn that Jesus was the desire of my heart. I would seek him and find him. He would fill me to the brim with the gospel of his love and mercy and lavishing grace.

PART II

PLUNGING INTO THE DEEP END OF GRACE

Chapter 6
Back to Sunday School

When I was in elementary school, I struggled with fear big-time. It was the '80s, and kidnapping was on the rise. Schools gave informational assemblies on how we could protect ourselves from kidnappers. Even mid-week services at church offered how-tos. It seemed we couldn't get away from the cultural hysteria around kidnapping and yet, I was hearing a different message at church that held up the idea that I should "fear not." But what if I had fear? What did that say about my faith?

During the summer after my sixth grade school year, I stayed at a friend's house while my parents worked during the day. Our friend's mom did daycare, and I would help. One day, she told her oldest son and me to go get milk at the local convenience store a few blocks away. They lived in a very busy area of the city, and we had to cross a sketchy intersection and walk through colorful neighborhoods to get to Cumberland Farms to get milk. I was wary and nervous when she asked, but I went. The whole time, I was scared that someone would grab us, and we would never make it back to her house.

That evening, I downloaded on my mom in tears and frustration that I could've been kidnapped that day. She talked with our friend about it, but my fears didn't cease. I remember ruining a backyard camp-out with my sister one night because the fear of being kidnapped consumed me.

When Mike and I got married, I was still fearful, but I covered it up pretty well. I was afraid my husband would die and leave me in a strange city to fend for myself. Or we'd have kids, and I wouldn't know what to do.

By the time Mike's mom passed away, Tullie was born, Eli passed away, and Ellison was born, I was a nervous wreck. I was waiting for the next bomb to drop. I knew beyond a shadow of a doubt that life was uncertain and that anything could happen. I would wake up in cold sweats with a bad dream or thoughts about some imagined situation that wouldn't let me rest. I knew that anything could happen, and I—Was—Scared.

I was scared that I would lose another kid. I was scared that my husband would die. I was scared that an emergency would happen to a family member on the East Coast, and I wouldn't make it in time. I was scared of accidents. I was scared of remodels. I was scared of a fatal illness. I was scared of anything happening, simply because I knew it could.

In 2009, a popular pastor was diagnosed with brain cancer, and he said, "I'm scared, but Jesus is enough for this." I laughed a cynical laugh. I didn't believe it. I remember telling Mike, "How can he say that? Would Jesus be enough for us? After all of this?" Mike's response, "You're breathing. We're breathing. He's proven that he is enough. Why wouldn't he be enough later?"

I had to think about that.

Each time I read "fear not" in the Bible, it seemed like a strong command. So, I reasoned that if I experienced fear, I was sinning. I could be at the top of a hill on a cliff and, if I feared that I would fall, I would be a sinner. Somehow, Jesus wouldn't save me or be enough for me. If I feared, then I didn't trust God. But I knew that I did trust him, or at least I was trying to trust amid my own uncertainty. I kept "giving" my fear to Jesus—"laying it at the cross," but the fear was still there. I wondered what I was doing wrong because it was difficult to calm my heart.

I was talking with a Seattle friend one day and she said, "Sometimes I need to remind myself of Sunday School songs. I need to sing the songs that I learned there because they can be the purest form of truth, and they're easy to remember." I laughed at her when she said it. But during a heated debate with a toddler, I quickly learned that he and I both needed Sunday School songs to be reminded of simple truths.

I had some serious Sunday School to do in my own life. I had thought that having a healthy baby would be a cure-all and mend all, but that wasn't the case. I was struggling and sinking in my fear, anxiety, pride, pain, envy, and my inability to "move on."

In May after Ellison was born, our church hosted Paul Tripp and Timothy Lane to do a seminar on their book *How People Change*. We got an overview of what the book was about over a couple of days. I stood in the back, holding Ellison and listening to the gospel, feeling like I was hearing it for the first time. I'm not an avid notetaker, so I just let the words pour over me as I listened to them talk about Jesus, suffering, fire, and the blessings and trials that people face. I knew that I needed Jesus, but I was fearful that he wouldn't truly be enough to see me through this.

As I listened, I started thinking that maybe God was good. At the time, I didn't think that God was good. At least not to me and my family. There had been too much tragedy in such a short amount of time for anyone to prove his goodness to me.

There was a song we sang in church, and the lyrics went like this: "For your goodness Lord. For the things you do. For your mercy and all of the ways you have been faithful to me." And each time the slides came up for that song, I would stand there stone-faced. He was not good. He had not been faithful to me. At least not in the way I thought he should have been good and faithful.

That's where I failed. I was basing his goodness and faithfulness on me. On my feelings. On my comfort. On my goodness. In my Sunday School, I learned that his goodness is not based on my happiness, my contentment or my lack of. His goodness is based on who he is, not on the circumstances around me.

Ellison was healthy. She also cried. A lot. Her only happy place was being held or eating. (Still is.) During my pregnancy with her, I had been terrified. Every moment without a kick or every weird feeling, I felt for sure that she would not make it. I was certain that I would not deliver a breathing baby. But I had delivered a breathing, hungry baby very ready to face the world. However, the fear wouldn't cease. I was terrified of SIDS. I feared that she could be taken without notice. I knew she was God's child only on loan to me, but the thought of burying another child terrified me. I was scared that if I connected with her, she would be taken away from me, so I kept as much distance as a mom could.

When she was about three months old, I wept, because I felt guilty. I apologized to her through tears as I held her one day. I knew I hadn't been holding her because I wanted to, I was holding her because she was crying, and she was only happy in my arms. She wasn't colicky. She didn't need anything extra. I needed her, and Jesus knew that. He knew that I had to hold her and love her and kiss her and spend the quiet of the night with her, lying next to her or rocking back and forth. Babies need their moms, but I really believe that I needed her. Jesus used her to help ease my fear. Her crying meant she was still breathing.

I was living in chronic fear, and I didn't think I could ever get out of it. None of the familiar verses such as Joshua 1:9 were working: *"Have I not commanded you? Be strong and courageous. Do not be frightened, and do not be dismayed, for the* Lord *your God is with you wherever you go."* If that was a command to not be afraid, I was failing miserably.

A year after we went to the *How People Change* training, I heard through the grapevine that my friend, Jackie was leading a group of ladies through the book. I emailed her and asked if I could hop in. Because it was such a large group, she divided us up geographically. We all lived near one another, at least within a few miles. We would meet in small groups and then meet as a larger group to go over the lesson for the coming week.

April 24, 2008 was the day before Eli's second birthday. I was determined to go to this study, sit, not say anything, and just listen. I didn't want to say anything, and I wasn't going to cry.

I made it through our small group portion unscathed. When we got to bigger group, a friend started to lead worship and played, "It Is Well." I thought that it was a cruel joke. We had played that song at Eli's service two years prior. However, I was determined not to cry.

Jackie started talking and, about 15 minutes into her talk, she began to read 2 Corinthians 4:16–18:

> *So we do not lose heart. Though our outer self is wasting away, our inner self is being renewed day by day. For this light momentary affliction is preparing for us an eternal weight of glory beyond all comparison, as we look not to the things that are seen but to the things that are unseen. For the things that are seen are transient, but the things that are unseen are eternal.*

I started to ugly cry. Sitting right there in my chair with people all around me, I ugly cried in a visible and ugly way. I was a mess! And I was mad! I was mad at God because didn't he know what day it was? Didn't he know what those verses and song meant? Didn't he know that I was barely holding on and that reminding me of why we chose those verses and song was just plain cruel? Didn't he know that it hurt to bury a son and celebrate a birthday without a person to show for it?

Jackie sweetly asked if she could pray for me. She knew. She knew why I was crying. I think maybe the timeline had come together in her head. I hadn't told her that it was coming, because ironically, I didn't want the attention. Jackie prayed. I hurt, and I was grasping at straws. I was desperate, and I was tired.

On the way home that day, a friend called to check in. She had played the harp and sang songs at Eli's service. I was pretty upset and still mad that God would bring up such precious things at a time when I was trying to forget. I relayed to her everything that happened. She listened quietly to me rant and at the end, she said, "I think that is beautiful. God is so sweet and kind. He is showing you that he remembers. He remembers your pain. Jesus is crying and groaning for you. He remembers you today. You are not alone." My only response, "Oh. I guess you're right."

When Mike came home, I told him what had happened. We had reservations to spend time away together for the next evening, and friends were going to watch the kids. I told him that something I thought was cruel had turned into something sweet—that God was kind. He remembered us.

Birthdays and anniversaries for a child or a loved one who has gone Home before us are weird. You know you're supposed to do something, but you don't know what to do. Their life is something that we should take the time to remember, but they aren't here, and it's hard to decide how to commemorate. After Eli's second birthday, I knew that I needed to learn the gospel.

I knew that I didn't have a "God" answer for everything. I didn't know why Mike's mom died so quickly. Why Tullie was born the way she was. Why Eli died. Why Tullie was on oxygen for what seemed like forever. Why we got pregnant with Ellison so quickly. Why the pregnancy was so difficult. Why? Why? Why? My list could go on and on. There are answers that I won't get. It's just the way it is. It doesn't mean that Jesus is less present or less sovereign. It just means I won't have answers. That's okay, but it took a while to come to terms with that.

One day during my Sunday School, I stripped my theology to the bare essentials. I went back to the basics. Jesus was born of a virgin. He died. He died for my sins. He rose again. He lives in heaven. He loves me. Then, I started rebuilding from there. I have to say my theology looks different than before. More mature. More put together. Simpler. More my own. More Jesus.

I cannot say that I am thankful for what my family has walked through, but I can say that I am thankful for Jesus. I am thankful for his death, his resurrection, his salvation. His gifts are so much more than I deserve. I'm thankful that he hasn't let go of his grip on me. Because without him, I would not be where I am. Even through my anger and frustration, my sadness and my grief, Jesus has been loving and patient.

> *I bless the* Lord *who gives me counsel; in the night also my heart instructs me. I have set the* Lord *always before me; because he is at my right hand,* ***I shall not be shaken****. Therefore my heart is glad, and my whole being rejoices;* ***my flesh also dwells secure.*** *For* ***you will not abandon my soul to Sheol****, or let your holy one see corruption.* ***You make known to me the path of life;*** *in your presence there is fullness of joy; at your right hand are pleasures forevermore* (emphasis mine).
>
> —Psalm 16:7–11

Sometimes, I felt pushed with Christian-ese and pressure to heal, to be where someone else thought that I should be. As if I was on a timeline. A lot of times, it was a pressure that I put on myself because I would hear a story about how someone else handled tragedy better.

I was at a women's retreat when Tullie was almost three and Ellison was still a baby. We were studying the book of Ephesians during the retreat. I was sitting at a table full of people that I had known for years, and Ephesians 1:18 came up: *"having the eyes of your hearts enlightened, that you may know what is the hope in which he has called you."* I spoke up and said, "I'm not even sure I believe in this hope. I don't know what it is, but I have none." I had hope when I was on bedrest that Eli would live. With each day, there had been hope. Then, there was none.

Later that evening a lady gave her testimony. She shared that her child was born still. She acknowledged that, yes, it was hard, but she was able to proclaim like Job, "Blessed be the name of the Lord" and worship while she held her stillborn child. I sat there and listened and thought, "I can't do that, and it's been nearly two years! I cannot proclaim his blessings. I don't have hope, and I don't feel blessed."

I was putting the pressure of her testimony on myself. I was comparing. I was thinking that somehow, I should have my act together, but that's not what Jesus does for us while we are walking in tragedy. He is patient and kind and loving. Prodding, yes, but usually he's so gentle that we don't know what has happened.

Meanwhile, Jesus was beginning to teach me about hope. Right after this retreat, Tullie was going to have her tonsils and adenoids removed. She had been on oxygen for three years. In the first 10 months, she was on it 24/7; after that, the oxygen was in our house for another two years and two months. After 10 months, she was on it for naps and for sleeping at night. When we brought her home from the NICU, we expected that the oxygen would be temporary, but with each appointment, we would have a step forward and then a step back for quite some time.

Many children with Down syndrome have cardiac issues. A lot of kids are born with holes in their hearts that need to be repaired. Tullie wasn't born with this, for which we are grateful, but the doctors wanted her on oxygen to protect her healthy heart. Each time her levels were low, her heart would start working harder because of the lack of oxygen, and she would retain too much carbon dioxide.

This would put pressure on her heart, and the muscle would grow another layer if it was working too hard. So, to be safe, the oxygen stayed with us for three years.

That oxygen became a symbol of hope to me. I felt that if I could get that oxygen out of the house, then things would change. It seemed to be the thing I held onto. With each doctor appointment, we got closer to being out of the oxygen world. Each time we went, we hoped that "just maybe this time, we'll leave without the tanks." But that didn't happen for a very long time.

When I went to the retreat, I had a warped idea of hope. I kept getting stuck on Ephesians 1:18, which says, *"having the eyes of your hearts enlightened, that you may know what is* ***the hope*** *to which he has called you, what are the riches of his glorious inheritance in the saints"* (emphasis mine). The hope to which he has called us. I had none, and I didn't know what the hope was that he had called us to, and that hope did not seem within my grasp, especially where the oxygen was concerned; that was something I couldn't control.

I was putting my hope in things that I could touch, and all the while I prayed, "Please Lord take the oxygen away; show me that you care about us. Show me that you can heal her in this." My prayer wasn't for my daughter to be healed, though I did want that. My prayer was more about being inconvenienced in my life. It was about me being free from equipment, so that I wouldn't have to look at it as a reminder that we were "that family." It was trusting in the hope of my desire being answered rather than in the hope of the cross. My desire was not God, dying to myself, or running after Jesus. My desire was trying to bring some sort of comfort back to my life that didn't involve medical equipment and having fewer doctor appointments.

I kept thinking that I had no hope because life had been beyond crazy for a good solid two years. We had experienced disappointment after disappointment. We had fight after fight. We had stress after stress. We had financial struggles. I had been thinking, "If this was gone. . . ." But it wasn't about the oxygen being gone. It wasn't about life getting better. It wasn't about our circumstances changing. It was the fact that I didn't know the *hope* Paul was talking about, and I would scoff at the idea that there really was such a thing.

I knew that I wouldn't turn my back on God altogether, but I also knew that I needed the hope that Paul talked about. I thought the lady who talked about her stillborn baby must've been a Super Christian if she believed what she said because I most certainly was not a Super Christian.

On the day that the oxygen finally left my house, I was on the phone with my mom telling her how excited I was. We were going to throw an Oxygen Party because we didn't have it in the house anymore. However, within a few minutes of that conversation, we were wondering whether my dad had suffered a stroke, and Mom was calling an ambulance. The elation that I thought I would have the day the oxygen left the house was overshadowed by my dad's health in a matter of minutes. The oxygen left, but hope did not replace it.

I never had an Oxygen Party. I really wanted one. I had big plans of inviting people over for food and drink and celebrating the oxygen not being in our house anymore. But we thought my dad had a stroke, so I raced back to Massachusetts to see him. We learned later that he had been clearing some trees and had been hit in the head with a branch, which caused his symptoms. It was nearly life threatening, but he made a full recovery for which we are all grateful.

I had thought that when the oxygen left the house, things would get better. My dad's accident was a cruel awakening that things would not magically get better. But we do that. We put our hope in people or in inanimate objects that we don't like having around, and we think, "If this just leaves, we'll be better. If this just leaves, my life will get more on track."

My hope was in the wrong place. My hope was in something that wasn't going to change my life all that much. My hope was not in

Jesus where it should have been. It was in my own selfishness trying to manage my own kingdom to make it better for myself.

What I needed was the hope that Paul describes in Ephesians 1:18–21:

> That ***you may know what is the hope to which he has called you****, what are the riches of his glorious inheritance in the saints, and what is the* ***immeasurable greatness of his power toward us who believe****, according to the working of his great might that he worked in Christ when he raised him from the dead and seated him at his right hand in the heavenly places, far above all rule and authority and power and dominion, and above every name that is named, not only in this age but also in the one to come* (emphasis mine).

Paul was talking about the hope of Jesus Christ—what Jesus did! What he conquered! He conquered death and through that he gave us an amazing inheritance **with** him in heaven. Therein lies our hope, not in things or the people of this world. They will surely fail us and will never satisfy. We will always be yearning for hope in that case.

In the fall of 2008, our church began a sermon series on Philippians: "*Rejoice in the Lord* ***always****; again I will say rejoice*" (Phil. 4:4, emphasis mine). I didn't like that verse much, because I didn't know how to rejoice in the *always*. I knew how to rejoice when the Patriots won the Super Bowl or the Red Sox won a World Series, but I couldn't rejoice too much beyond that. I could not rejoice in my life at the moment.

Before each sermon, they showed short documentary videos about the authors of well-known hymns such as "Amazing Grace,"

"It Is Well with My Soul," "Solid Rock," and others. They would talk about how difficult and arduous the lives of the composers had been. Many of their lives had been full of sickness and death, and the words of their songs were full of joy and groaning. There is an authenticity in those hymns that is raw, powerful, and wonderful. With each story and sermon, I began to understand more of suffering and the gospel. I began to understand suffering and Jesus.

We had never heard teaching about suffering like we did in Seattle. *Suffering* was a word that people used regularly. People talked more openly about their pain. We knew people who had suffered greatly from abuse, physical pain, abandonment, and in some situations, spiritually abusive relationships.

My takeaway from Philippians and what I am still learning is to *"Rejoice in the Lord always; again I will say, rejoice."* In Philippians 4:4, rejoicing is a command. It's not Paul requesting that we consider an idea; it's a command, an imperative. You! Rejoice! Always! You! Not when we feel like it when we get good news about a job. Rejoice always. When we get the cancer diagnosis. Rejoice always, when we get the positive pregnancy test. Rejoice always, when our children go into the arms of Jesus too soon. Rejoice always, when we get a clean bill of health. Rejoice always, when we discover a cheating spouse. Rejoice always, when there is no money in the bank. Rejoice always, when the bank is overflowing. Rejoice always, when the oxygen leaves the house and Dad has a life threatening accident in the same day. Rejoice. Always.

We are not rejoicing because of our circumstances. Circumstances can and will change, and they can change quickly. We are rejoicing in who our Lord is. He is unchanging. He is perfect. He is constant. He holds the planets in their place, and he can hold our circumstances as well. We are rejoicing that he is faithful. He is true. He purchased our salvation with his own life. He conquered death, and this life is not all there is. We rejoice because he is our hope, joy, and peace; he loves us with an unending, everlasting love. He holds us. Nothing is a surprise to him. He knows.

I had been raised in church. I had gone to youth group. I had started a Bible club in my high school. I had gone on mission trips, minored in Bible in college, and had read the Bible several times, but I was just beginning to learn about Jesus.

I was in Sunday School daily learning the gospel for what seemed to be the first time. I was hoping, rejoicing, trusting, and learning to be content in who Jesus is and what he accomplished on the cross. But I was also learning to live in the tension that the world is unfair, and that life is deeply painful and full of uncertainty and fear.

If I believe Jesus is completely human and was sent in order to understand us and be like us, then I must believe that he struggled just as I have. That he suffered deeply. That he felt fear, betrayal, pain, and frustration. He experienced all those emotions at the Garden of Gethsemane before his death. He felt fear like I have felt fear, and yet he did not allow fear to consume him. I can't even imagine that.

He died for my fear and anxiety. He died for my frustrations and my lack of hope. He died for death, so that I no longer need to fear it. So, now I know that the words of Luke 12:32 are not trite: *"Fear not, little flock, for it is your Father's good pleasure to give you the kingdom."* Through his death and resurrection, he has given us the kingdom, and we have no reason to fear.

Chapter 7

Bear One Another's Burdens

Bear one another's burdens, and so fulfill the law of Christ.

—Galatians 6:2

I learned Galatians 6:2 in Missionettes (a version of Girl Scouts hosted by the Assemblies of God) when I was growing up. The verse was a quick one to learn and it stuck with me. It has a good beat to it too. As we were experiencing suffering, this verse kept coming to mind. I didn't always feel like my burdens were being lifted within our church community. In time, I felt very isolated in my pain. Relationships felt tricky. What I have realized in hindsight, however, that we had people who stuck it out with us. They were grieving and mourning with us and were the ones who helped whenever we needed, and we did the same for them.

Relationships change as time goes on. I'm not close friends with the people that I grew up with. We got married and moved far away from one another. Our paths didn't cross again for years. It wasn't because of a tragedy; it's just the way it is.

During my family's time in Seattle though, our friendships grew stronger. We were doing life with people and raising our kids together. But the more life threw at us, the lonelier I felt. We were serving each Sunday and each week in our home with Community Groups. But I continually felt that no one was bearing my burdens. Each time I read Galatians 6:2, I would laugh out a cynical snort and disbelieve that it was real.

We received a lot of meals during our tough times. Friends babysat our kids when we had appointments. We had been served, and we were grateful, but I felt that my burdens had not been carried by someone else.

I had a friend, and our two older children were a couple of months a part. Our two youngest would have been a couple of months apart, but Eli had gone Home. She had recently had a baby, and there was a weekly playdate that a group of moms attended. One week, I had my kids dressed and ready to go, but at the last second, I decided to stay home. I couldn't bear to see my friend and her baby. I called to tell her not to wait for me. She said in a chipper voice, "Come on! Come! You should get out! You need to cheer up." She kept pushing until I finally said, "I can't see your baby. I don't want to see her, and I'm staying home." I knew my words hurt her, and that conversation may have been the beginning of the end of our friendship. But seeing my friend's happiness was hard for me. I felt cheated. It was unfair that she had her baby, but I didn't have mine.

The fact is, friendships change over the years. Sometimes, tragedy can change relationships quickly. This friendship died a slow death. Maybe the relationship died because of me, or maybe it was her. Most likely, it was both of us. We were both in our 20s. We were young mothers who couldn't navigate grief well, so we "helped" each other by creating temporary distance and never reconciled. It was too hard to fight for our friendship at the time, and there were other things that seemed more pressing for both of us. I was hurt and angry and kept venting to Mike about how friends don't treat one another like this—that we're supposed to stick closer than a brother and push through life, but some friends simply can't. I have learned over the years that it's okay to let go of people who can't remain in the hard seasons of other people's lives. Maybe they were made to stick it out with someone else, just not me.

One day when Tullie was three, a lady from church put up a question on our church's website asking if there were any other families with special needs kids. A few of us popped up with a hearty "Yes!" Within a week, a parent group was formed, and plans were made to meet, share, and talk. It was a sweet, honest, raw, humbling, and wonderful time. It refreshed my soul in important ways, and I realized I needed this newfound community. I thought we'd experienced community before, but we didn't know any other families who had faced the challenges and difficulty of raising a child with a disability, until then.

There were parents in that group who had children diagnosed with Coffin-Siris syndrome, hearing loss, a heart transplant, CHARGE syndrome, Autism, and Turrets syndrome. Our children's disabilities may have been different, but we had two things in common: We loved Jesus, and we were desperate for community with others facing the task of raising special needs children. We met once a month for three or four years, and it was a breath of fresh air for all of us. People from that group talk periodically, but life has gotten busy since then. The timing of the group coming together had been perfect for each of us. We were all drowning in our own experiences, and Jesus put us together when we needed one another most. Some very sweet friendships were formed.

I also learned something very valuable. All our kids are so different and so special. Some families have an exceptionally difficult task when their child is frequently sick and hospitalized, shuttling back and forth to endless doctor appointments. I've learned to ask myself what can be done to help families in situations like this. Sometimes, we must be sensitive to not step on people's toes and force our way into their lives. But other times, that's necessary when we see a family suffering so badly.

Jesus used that community of ladies to save me. To encourage me, cry with me, to love on our family during surgeries, pregnancies, and grief. I'm so grateful for them. I hope that they feel the same way.

During the *How People Change* study, I was a good wreck. I had mentioned before that our leader, Jackie, put us in groups geographically. Everyone in my group lived within a few miles of each other.

On the morning of November 16, 2009, a new friend from the group, Liz, called, sobbing, and asked if I could watch her toddler, because her daughter had died in utero. Liz and her husband dropped off their toddler and rushed off to the hospital to be induced. During the next 24 hours, their daughter and I got a crash course in learning about each other, and after the kids were in bed, I went to the hospital to see Liz and her husband. When you have already buried a child, you'd think you'd know what to say, but you don't. Walking with someone who is experiencing a similar tragedy is like having bandages ripped off a scabbing sore that still bleeds.

I sat with Liz and her husband that night for a while during her labor. When I came home from the hospital that evening, I got into bed with Mike and began to weep for our friends and for myself. Later, in the wee hours of the morning, Liz's daughter and I hung out with *Thomas the Train*, and I prayed for Liz while Thomas droned in the background.

While Liz was giving birth to a stillborn baby girl, we found out later that same evening another lady in church was giving birth to a stillborn baby boy. I couldn't reach out to her that evening because emotionally and physically, I had been stretched thin. A few weeks later, though I stopped by Mandy's house and asked if she and Liz wanted to meet up at my house after the holidays were over.

After Liz returned from Ohio after the holidays, she and Mandy agreed to come over one Monday morning in January 2010. For the next year, Liz and Mandy sat at my kitchen table every Monday morning. We talked about our pain. We shared our fears. We talked about shoes. Ate breakfast and formed a beautiful friendship. We were three ladies who had experienced deep loss and learned to support and love one another. I've realized I cannot give my friends ultimate comfort, only the God of heaven can do that. I can continue to pray and intercede for them, yes, but it cannot weigh heavily on me.

> *Blessed be the God and Father of our Lord Jesus Christ, the Father of mercies and God of all comfort, who comforts us in all our affliction, so that we may be able to comfort those who are in any affliction, with the comfort with which we ourselves are comforted by God. For as we share abundantly in Christ's sufferings, so through Christ we share abundantly in comfort too. If we are afflicted, it is for your comfort and salvation; and if we are comforted, it is for your comfort, which you experience when you patiently endure the same sufferings that we suffer. Our hope for you is unshaken, for we know that as you share in our sufferings, you will also share in our comfort.*
>
> —2 Corinthians 1:3–7

Learning to share our painful experiences and struggles with others who had experienced tragedy or were caring for a child with disabilities encouraged me. We pointed one another to Jesus during our conversations. He is the Author and Perfecter of our faith, even when we struggled to believe on the dark days. In those moments around my kitchen table, we pointed one another to Jesus, our sole source of comfort and the one we desperately needed.

My time in these groups with these friends reminds me of Romans 1:11–12, *"For I long to see you, that I may impart to you some spiritual gift to strengthen you—that is, that we may be mutually encouraged by each other's faith, both yours and mine."* Paul wanted to see the Romans so they could encourage one another. I get a picture in my head of Paul and a small church congregation sitting in someone's home around a kitchen table sharing life together, both good and bad. The difficulties and sadness of life and God's faithfulness and kindness. Rome was not a place where Christians were loved and cared for, so they had a lot to talk about. I can say with confidence that each of the ladies I spent time with encouraged me.

I read a book by Kelle Hampton, about her experience of parenting a daughter with Down syndrome. She kept mentioning the amazing friends she had. I found myself envious of her. I didn't think I had amazing friends; I had felt abandoned. I felt like I was grieving alone because no one understood what I was going through. But I was very wrong. I had friends who stuck with me even when I wasn't sticking with them. They walked with me through fire by planning services, delivering meals, babysitting, being good listeners even when distance separated us. My friends taught me the gospel when I was too blind to see it and too hurt to hear it.

> *"Bear one another's burdens, and so fulfill the **law of Christ**"* (emphasis mine).
>
> —Galatians 6:2

> *"A* ***new commandment I give to you, that you love one another****: just as I have loved you, you also are to love one another. By this all people will know that you are my disciples, if you have love for one another"* (emphasis mine).
>
> —John 13:34–35

The "law of Christ" is loving other people. When we walk with people in their grief, suffering, and sin, we are bearing their burdens and fulfilling the law of Christ. But it is hard! It means getting into muddy, messy grime and walking with them in thick ever-shifting sludge. My most valuable friendships are the ones in which people have walked with me and I with them through the darkest days of our lives. They have loved well.

Truly bearing one another's burdens is not for the weak of heart, but it is a command for the Christian to love those who are suffering and their neighbors well.

Chapter 8
Breather

A college friend and I were catching up on the phone one day. She is the mother of 10 children, but only three are living. Seven of her children went Home to be with Jesus before her. She shared how she had expressed to a friend how difficult her grief process had been. And her friend replied by saying, "Lean into Jesus because when you do you receive more strength." Immediately, my heart broke. Truly.

I had heard this sort of message when someone tried to comfort me, too. When someone says, "Lean into Jesus," I think, "But I am. I am so desperate. What else do I have to do to feel better?" Why do we say things like that? Sure, it's an attempt to comfort, but Jesus never said, "If you lean into me more, then I'll help you." It's another Christian karma statement. Do this. Get that.

But abiding in Jesus is altogether different. Abiding is defined by *Merriam-Webster* dictionary as "continuing without change; enduring; steadfast." Leaning is defined as "inclination; tendency."

In John 15, Jesus talks about us abiding in him and him abiding in us. It is a two-way street, but it is steadfast. He is steadfast. When we belong to him, the abiding is unchanging. It continues no matter life's circumstances. Paul confirms in Ephesians 3 and Romans 8 that nothing can separate us from the love of God. Nothing. By the time Ellison was three, I was beginning to understand the abiding idea. That Jesus was for me, had died for me, and was enough. I was beginning to believe I couldn't do any more to get him.

Liz and Mandy came to my house every Monday for a year. Our kitchen conversations continued throughout our pregnancies. Mandy had moved, but Liz lived only a couple of miles away, so our friendship became more than just relating over a shared experience. We became rich friends very quickly. We shared sushi, wine, tacos, coffee, babysitting, necklaces, and a lot of conversations and laughter.

My pregnancy with our sixth child, a boy, was moving along swimmingly (I had a miscarriage after Ellison was born). But this pregnancy was boring and uneventful for which we were all grateful. One evening, I was making dinner and our oldest son, Josiah, was doing his homework at the kitchen table. He looked up at me out of the blue and said, "Mom, I am going to love God even if all of my family is taken away or if they die." I looked up at him and stopped stirring the chili that was on the stove. I walked over to him and held his face in my hands, and I said, "I love that you are saying this. Don't forget. Don't forget how much Jesus loves you. Don't forget that he died for you. Don't forget that life will be hard. Remember this moment. Remember these words when things get hard."

In Josiah's seven years of life, he had lost a brother, and he had a sister with special needs. (I found out later that he met her on the playground every morning to check in on her during recess.) I recognized that life had just started for him. He hadn't even become an adult yet! My desire for him is to keep loving God even in the hardest, most broken places of life. To know the gospel and to cling to its promises.

Boston Samuel Bates was born on February 25, 2011. He was born smiling. He was ready to cozy up and to snuggle. He was a son that seemed to fill in a longing void. Our family felt whole. Complete.

We had always wanted to travel as a family and show our kids the country. So, when Boston was four months old, we hopped into a motor home with bunk beds, rented out our house, and hit the road. We left in June and spent the whole summer in the northern states. Across the plains, and the Midwest. We made our way to the Northeast in late summer and early fall. We traveled down the East Coast in October and were hanging out in Florida by Thanksgiving. Christmas was spent on the Gulf Coast. By spring, we got to California and rolled back into Seattle in May 2012. We joked about "chasing the sun for a year," because it seemed we had been without it for eleven years living in Seattle.

On our trip, we went to Acadia National Park; Disney World; and Washington, DC. We hiked the Blue Ridge Mountains and saw the Grand Canyon, Pacific Ocean, Legoland, Redwood Forest, and Petrified Forest. We visited family and friends all over the country, making new friends along the way. We enjoyed one another. Our kids grew, and our children met our friends' children. We spent time with family we rarely see. We laughed and cried with friends, and we visited all kinds of churches.

That trip was refreshing. There were stressful parts too, like when the slide in the motor home broke, and someone (me) didn't close a back window all the way, and the wind took it while we were driving. At one point, the turbo went out on the engine. Boston had a double ear infection, influenza, and pink eye, and all we wanted to do was go home. Those were random moments and days, but the other 350 days were filled with different things to see and do. We lived on our own time schedule (the best we could, Mike still had to work) for a year. We did what we wanted, went where we wanted, and hung out with whomever we chose.

Before we started packing for the trip, I asked Mike if we could bring Eli with us. I asked almost hesitantly. Somehow thinking that it would be taking up too much room to have the urn and memory box with us. Mike looked at me and said, "Of course." I could pack up my wedding pictures. My furniture. My old college pictures. Yearbooks. Sentimental keepsakes. The other kids "special items" and put them into storage, but I couldn't pack up Eli's urn and memory box.

I'm so glad we kept it with us. Throughout the months we were traveling, some of our friends "met" our son through the pictures and keepsakes in the memory box, and I'm so grateful we were able to share that with them. But with all those moments, nothing was as sweet as the memory of sharing Eli with our other children.

I was folding laundry one day when Ellison went to a cabinet that Mike and I had recently cleaned and opened it up. She saw Eli's urn right there, and it was easy to grab. She grabbed it and said, "This is my brother! Can we open it so I can see him?" I said, "We can't open it, but I'll show you his pictures when I'm done with this laundry." She said, "Ok!"

While she went skipping away back to the table with Josiah and her daddy, I thought, "I was so not ready for this today."

As she came walking back to the bedroom, I was finishing up the laundry. Meanwhile, the three older kids had already started a conversation about seeing pictures of Eli and talking about where Eli was at that very moment. I pulled out the pictures, and the kids looked at each one. We looked at prints of his hands and his feet. We looked at pieces of hair from his head. We looked at the bracelets from the hospital and the blood pressure cuffs and the smallest, ittiest, bittiest, littlest diapers that you've ever seen. The kids marveled at how tiny he was.

The kids were so matter of fact. "That's my brother." "He's with God." We're going to be with God and him one day."

Boston even army crawled his way into the conversation and while I held onto him, I looked at pictures of Eli, and it struck me that I was surrounded by all six of my children (as well as remembering a miscarriage a couple of years prior). Each one a blessing.

Each one in Jesus's grasp. One with Jesus already. Four here that we could touch, hold, and watch grow and mature. It was a tender, overwhelming moment—being surrounded by all four soft-hearted, teachable kids. One moment we were talking about how God made Adam out of dirt and the next how Jesus died for us so we can be in heaven with him when we die if we believe in him.

These are the moments we look for as parents. The times when our children's hearts are pliable and we're able to be raw and honest about our own painful experiences. These are the times when our children see us as real and vulnerable. That is when Jesus is glorified. When we show our children where our hope lies.

I'm glad we brought Eli with us even if it was just for that conversation with the other children. One day, it will be our turn to be with Jesus and be reunited with our son and brother. Our tears and pain will be washed away and will be no more (Isa. 25:8 and Rev. 21:4). Instead, there will be rejoicing and dancing. It will be a sweet, wonderful, and perfect moment.

During our trip, Tullie and Boston formed a sweet relationship. Tullie and Boston would get up before us, and we'd wake up to the sounds of the two of them playing games in his bed on the other side of our wall. They would be giggling and laughing. Tullie would make up stories to tell Boston. It was truly a wonderful memory I will hold onto forever. Their relationship carried on when we got home. She was always extra protective of him.

We had a great trip, but it was good to get back to Seattle. We moved back into our house and picked up where we had left off. Mike continued working from home, and we reconnected with our friends. But being back in Seattle reminded us of the financial stress of living in an expensive city. Things were simply too expensive, and we couldn't travel anymore, so we decided to look around the country for a cheaper place to live.

We like the top two corners (the Northeast and the Pacific Northwest), and we kept our search to those areas, because we liked them. We looked all over eastern Washington, the Peninsula, Northern Oregon and the northern part of western Washington. We looked back at the East Coast, but everything we could afford was built in 17 hundred something and needed several years of remodeling. So, one day Mike said, "What if we looked in the middle? After all, traveling to the top two corners will go much quicker in the RV! We'll split up our time! We'll go to Seattle one summer and go to New England the next! If we're in the middle, we'll get there in half the time!" We did. We looked in the middle.

We found a 40-acre property with rolling hills, outbuildings, a farmhouse, and farm equipment that us "city kids" didn't know how to use in Humansville (Yes, it is a real place.), Missouri. We sold what we didn't need. We packed up our motor home, a U-Haul truck, and we moved to Humansville in July 2014.

We had been in Humansville for six months when Mike got a serious headache that put him in bed for a whole morning. During this headache, he felt like he had a vision of sorts. He got up and wrote down everything he had on his heart. He was bothered by it because it seemed like a really big task. He was called to love and serve Humansville by employing others.

My husband is an entrepreneur. The summer we dated in Massachusetts, Mike bought and sold two motorcycles, and he was always looking for a good deal. We've owned multiple businesses throughout our marriage. Mike has an eye for knowing value and how to make a good deal. My parents said that they knew with Mike, we would always make it financially. We have, but we have also had some tight months and years. So, when Mike got his vision, he knew he needed a location to build a business in. We just didn't know what or where that would be.

There was an inn for sale about two miles away from us. It sits on a major intersection, has eight rooms and had been empty for six to nine months. The inn sits on five acres and has a huge shop on the property. We looked at it on New Year's Day 2015 and put in a full-price offer.

Through a series of many miracles, we were able to purchase the inn in February 2015. In April of that year, we opened a remodeled inn and named it The BarnwooD Inn, just in time for rodeos and the racetrack, fishing, and hunting seasons.

We had no idea what we were doing, but we learned. We watched hours of *Hotel Impossible.* We believed that if we could figure out what *not* to do, then we'd be okay. We listened to feedback and learned along the way. We fixed things that were wrong, and we are currently running a 5-star rated inn. We have repeat customers and new guests every year who love to stay here.

By the fall of 2015, we thought we were going at a pretty good clip. We were figuring things out, and we had a routine down, but then our world was about to be ripped apart. Again.

No amount of leaning on my part would make things better. Jesus is unchanging. He is secure, and we are as close as we can be in him. He is holding us despite our not "feeling" it. He is enduring and steadfast despite our circumstances. No matter how bad they are.

Chapter 9

Hadn't We Suffered Enough?

It seems to be commonplace that when a person has suffered a great deal, they are described as someone who has "suffered like Job." The whole book of Job in the Bible is about one man's great suffering and his great faith. Suffering, because he lost everything. Crops, children, animals, and money. Faith, because he continued to praise God for it despite never knowing the reason for his suffering. I had several people tell me to go read Job after we began to suffer greatly. I think it was their way of not having words of comfort to say and assuming that the book of Job would fill any void I had. It seems to be the go-to book of the Bible for sufferers.

I tried. I tried to read Job after Tullie was born and Eli passed away. I only got through the first few chapters and then I got annoyed with his friends. I couldn't plow through. I was going to have to take it up again later.

It's interesting though that there are 66 books in the Bible and each book touches on suffering and grief. Every single one. In some way, suffering or hardship is described. Why is it that folks say to a sufferer, "Go read Job"? Because he suffered the most? I beg to differ. Jesus suffered more.

One day in September 2015, Boston was playing, and he said, "Mom, I want five birthdays. **Five**!" He held up his hand showing off his five fingers. "Five!" I leaned over and gave him a hug and I said, "I want you to have five birthdays!"

His birthday wasn't until February, but he was excited. He would proclaim his desire for five birthdays on a regular basis. I couldn't promise five birthdays because I'm not God and I already knew that life was fleeting. So, my response was always the same, "I want you to have five birthdays, Boston!"

A couple of months after we moved to the inn, a man came rolling into our parking lot. The alternator in his car was dying as he rolled into a parking space. Mike went out to meet him, and the two of them hopped into our car and went down to the auto parts store. The man stayed in our inn for the evening and paid Mike to change out the alternator. We fed him breakfast, talked about Jesus, and shared stories. Come to find out, he was a father to seven kids, and we talked about maybe doing something together as families as they only lived two hours away up in Kansas City.

Several months went by, and we didn't hear from him. One day he contacted Mike and said that he and his family were going down to Branson and wondered if they could stay the night at our inn and we could all do something together as families. Mike, of course, said yes and as the day was approaching, we started planning our activities of eating food and visiting a local drive-through cave.

The morning of October 20, 2015, Mike took the day off work (He still had a day job that was paying the bills.) because our visitors were coming that day. We were cleaning up around the outside of the inn. I was cleaning the house; the kids were helping Mike outside, cleaning their rooms, playing with one another, hopping to obedience and using kind words. I remember cooking lunch, as we were waiting for our company, thinking, "Wow, everyone is so nice today." The sun was shining in the windows. It was a beautiful day.

Our four-year-old, Boston, was running past me to go play and stopped in his tracks and turned around and said, "Mom, I need to hug you. I love you." I responded, "Oh, Boston, I love you so much! Thanks for the hug!" He gave me a hug and a kiss on the cheek and took off to go play. I smiled and carried on with my work cleaning up and making lunch. All the while thinking, "Wow, this really is such a peaceful morning."

All our children were playing with Legos together on the living room floor and Mike came in and said, "Hey, guys I need some help picking up trash outside. Come on and let's get it done! Our friends are almost here." Each child stood up and went to get their shoes on. Boston was the first out the door.

I was cooking at the stove that faced the open front door that was letting the fall air come in the house. I heard Mike's truck start and begin to back up. Then I heard the scream. Mike screaming to call 911. Yelling. Holding Boston in his arms. Bloodied. Walking over to the side of the house, where our other children couldn't look out the window and see the horror playing out in our front yard.

There was an accident. Just out the front door on what seemed to be a perfect morning. Minutes after laughter. Minutes after excitement and expectation.

The other kids hadn't made it outside yet. They were still getting their shoes on. I pulled the curtains and made them stay inside. I will never forget Mike's yell. I will never forget screaming into the phone for the ambulance to hurry. For them to get here to save our son. The 911 operator was telling us what to do to breathe life back into his little body. A police officer came and stood over us, telling Mike to continue doing what he was doing, but as the two of us knelt over Boston's body, his breath had already been whisked away.

Meanwhile, our company pulled into our parking lot. They got out and stood in the distance and began to pray for our son to be revived, but Boston wasn't reviving. He was already in the arms of Jesus. That day, another son went Home.

We don't know what Boston was doing behind the truck. We don't know if he was trying to climb the tire and then tried to get out of the way. But Mike checked his mirrors and didn't see anything, and Boston was out of the line of the mirrors. When Mike backed up, he accidentally backed over our son. Our boy, who was full of life just moments before, died instantly.

A neighbor took me to the hospital following the ambulance and, as I was pacing the waiting room, someone came to take us to the "Bad News Room." I knew in my gut before the doctor came in that my son was Home, but she told me that they tried everything. They couldn't revive him. He had died.

Some can cry right away when they hear the horrific news; others are in so much shock that it takes a while for the events to sink in. I was the latter. I sat there, knowing. I sat there, frozen.

Word was getting out, and people we knew started to come to the hospital. A friend called my dad, because I couldn't.

When Mike got to the hospital, I told him the news that he already knew. The social worker asked if we wanted to go say good-bye to our son. He had not been alone. Someone had been sitting with him, and as we walked in, he quietly left.

If I had known that the hug I received from Boston not even two hours earlier would be my last, I would have clung to his four-year-old body longer. I would've soaked in his smell and touched his curls and gazed into his big blue eyes. But now, our son was cold and lifeless laying on a hospital bed. Mike and I held hands then stood on each side of the bed and held his hands and wept over him as we touched his hair and kissed his cheeks one last time. No parent should ever go through this. Ever.

When we got back to the "Bad News Room," our pastor was there. We sat down on the sofa, held one another, and cried out to Jesus. We had prayed in our parking lot for Jesus to save Boston. That was not his plan. Instead, we sat there and groaned to our Savior again. Another son, Home before us. Crying together. This loss felt so much more tragic simply because it was. This wasn't supposed to be.

We prayed with an undisputable knowledge of Truth, aching to believe it. We prayed with an affirmation of *knowing* that Jesus was enough, even though we were struggling to believe it at that moment. We prayed knowing but also aching for the security of his sovereignty and his love for us despite the immense pain we felt that day that is still with us. The pain that is still with us more than three years later.

I struggle with this sounding trite. That I sound like the woman who claimed to praise God while holding her son born still. Was I praising God? Maybe? Can we praise God while we groan and cry? I believe David did. During all his suffering, he'd cry out to God and ask why and then say, "Your steadfast love endures forever." Did I believe that his steadfast love endures forever in the "Bad News Room"? Yes. I did. I believed through aches and groans, and I believed through tears of shock and awe as I asked Jesus to protect my other children's hearts. Romans 8:26 rang in my ears: *"Likewise the Spirit helps us in our weakness. For we do not know what to pray for as we ought, but the Spirit himself intercedes for us with groanings too deep for words."*

All we could do was groan. When we returned home, all we could do was groan. When the tears dried up for the day, all we could do was groan. As we called friends in Seattle, all we could do was groan.

For the next several days, I believe the Spirit held us and groaned for us because we could not do it. Somehow, we got up out of bed each day. Friends and family came. The service was put together. Boston was cremated because I couldn't handle seeing a child's casket. We saw people we didn't plan to see. People traveled from all over the country to be with us. They groaned with us too. There were simply no words.

I believe that some of the hardest parts of grief in a tragic loss are the what-ifs. What if we hadn't met the man who needed his alternator fixed? If we hadn't met him, we wouldn't have been cleaning things up and moving vehicles. What if I had forced the kids to stay in and pick up the house rather than pick up outside? What if Boston hadn't given me that hug behind the sofa? Would he still be here if we hadn't had that moment?

What if I had made the kids get their schoolwork done that day rather than helping around the house and playing so nicely? What if the kids had been fighting and had not been kind? Maybe Boston would still be here. I can get myself lost in the what-ifs. They can consume me until I go mad. Sometimes, I want to because I want to see how something can be different. I *want* something to be different, but that can't be. And those what-ifs don't do anything except cause self-pity to dwell in my heart. There are days I want to sit in self-pity and the what-ifs because it's comfortable there, but it's also cold and lonely.

> *I am weary with my moaning; every night I flood my bed with tears; I drench my couch with my weeping. My eye wastes away because of grief; it grows weak because of all of my foes.*
>
> —Psalm 6:6–7

> *The Lord is my chosen portion and my cup, you hold my lot.*
>
> —Psalm 16:5

I know that King David understands. I read these verses over and over. Regularly. On the hard days, I read them.

I had started thinking about God's grace in tragedy and trying to find pieces of it with Mike's mom passing away, Tullie being born, my extended bedrest and Eli going Home. I had started a mental list over the years. Remembering the events and then Jesus would remind me of his grace with meals delivered, parents staying, an amazing insurance plan, childcare, and other random things.

But now? After "The Accident"? How can God be gracious through something so horrific? We had to come back to the place of The Accident after The Accident. We lived there! Evidence of God's Grace that day:

- We got home, and our visitors were still there. Our children had children to play video games with.
- My Aunt Kathy stayed with us all night until my parents and sister could get there the next day. She took care of us.
- A friend came over at 5:30 the next morning to sit with us.
- Everyone picked up the phone when I called them to share the news.
- Our kids remember their brother alive, not bloodied and lifeless.
- People took our kids to the park while we finished up the hospital responsibilities.
- Amid the chaos, there was peace.
- There were sweet memories from the morning.

God's grace is evident in tragedy. It's hard to see it at the time, but it is. He is present. His Son is with us and weeping with us while we weep. Years before I learned the gospel, I didn't think that God's grace was evident in tragedy. I just thought he left us to fend for ourselves, but he doesn't. He is in it. He is with us, and he weeps.

"I say to the Lord, 'You are my Lord; I have no good apart from you.'"

—Psalm 16:2

In November after The Accident, we put our three kids in the motor home and went to Massachusetts for Thanksgiving. The trip had already been planned, so we just continued with it. It was now a trip of sorrow as we tried to figure out how to regain our footing.

We wondered if we even could. While we were in Massachusetts, Mike and I went to Marblehead for the weekend. As we were walking around the town, I mentioned to Mike that even though we were in so much pain and chaos, I felt peaceful. Philippians 4:7 had become real, *"And the peace of God, which surpasses all understanding, will guard your hearts and your minds in Christ Jesus."* Peace didn't seem possible with what was going on around us. But I felt peaceful.

I had been studying the theme of the armor of God with our church before The Accident, and I noticed something in Ephesians 6:10–20 where Paul lays it all out. Paul begins listing out the armor in verses 14–18:

> *Stand therefore, having fastened on the belt of truth, and having put on the breastplate of righteousness, and, as shoes for your feet, having put on the readiness given by the gospel of peace. In all circumstances take up the shield of faith, with which you can extinguish all the flaming darts of the evil one; and take the helmet of salvation, and the sword of the Spirit, which is the word of God, praying at all times in the Spirit, with all prayer and supplication.*

Look at how Paul lists the armor. Truth is first. I believe there's a reason for that. Truth is the middle of the armor. It's the core. Truth holds up everything else. We can't "put on" or "carry" anything else without the core to help hold it all up.

The *"peace that surpasses understanding,"* which Paul writes about in Philippians 4, is unattainable without knowing truth. We all want peace. We try hard to have peace. I have an essential oil called Peace that I use when I'm feeling anxious or stressed out. We do breathing exercises to calm down and to get more peaceful. We talk to counselors and do yoga. We take walks through the woods and sit by lakes to feel peaceful. But that is faux peace. True peace only comes from knowing and believing truth. Knowing and believing the truth of the gospel and what Jesus has done for us.

I am not saying that since The Accident, we have not wept, gotten angry, yelled at our children, or felt like things were an utter mess. I have called or texted friends and asked them to tell me the gospel to remind me of Truth because I have felt like I had forgotten it. I am weak and broken. It is only by Jesus's amazing grace that he has held us and reminded us of his peace. He is enough.

We have always believed in organ donation. Our son, Josiah, just received his permit, and he chose to be an organ donor as well. The little donor logo has followed me for 26 years. It's something that we believe in because we believe in life. We believe in life at conception. We believe in life through foster care and adoption. We believe in life for the sick if we can help and if that help is in the donation of an organ of a deceased family member, we would donate.

We have friends whose daughter was born with a serious heart defect. They knew in utero that her heart was upside down and backwards. They knew that she would not have a chance at life unless there was a donation of a heart soon after her birth. That donation of a heart, however, meant that some parents were going to be without their baby that they had prayed and longed for. A baby that may have died unexpectedly. The family who gave the donation of that vital organ would experience a tragic loss more than they would experience the exhilaration of a life saved.

When I met my friend and she started talking about how her daughter received her heart, I asked her one day over coffee if she ever got in touch with the donors. Her response was that they had tried, but they didn't want to communicate. (All the correspondence goes through the donor agency, so there is no direct contact with the donors or recipients, unless both parties agree.) She had wondered if they ever would, but she also understood the complexity of the situation. It isn't as clear-cut as the movie *Return to Me* starring Minnie Driver and David Duchovany. Movies make life seem so easy. Sometimes.

After The Accident, we knew that we had a very healthy four-year-old with excellent organs. He could help someone, but in the hustle of trying to save his life, we missed the opportunity for major organs. When we brought it up to the nursing staff and doctors, it was too late; however, we were able to donate his eyes, cartilage, bone, and skin.

The donation agency called a day after The Accident to make sure we approved, and I answered all their questions robotically. Yes. No. Yes. Ok. Thank you. Bye.

But then when I got off the phone I couldn't get out of my head, they said, "We were able to take what we needed. It will help so many people." My son's body had been taken apart. Someone had taken the skin off. Someone had taken his eyes out. Someone had taken the cartilage from his kneecaps and elbows and wherever else. His body was being shared, and other people around the world would use it. Pieces of him would be everywhere. But I wanted his whole person here, with me. Where it was supposed to be.

The picture in my head was disgusting and sickening. My heart hurt more that my baby would literally be taken apart. I knew that it was for a good cause. I knew that his soul was at Home, and his body was merely a vehicle for him to use during his time on earth, but those pieces of his body? Those were the eyes that smiled at me. Those were the eyes that cried when he was sad. Those were the biggest, bluest eyes that I had ever seen. Those were the arms and legs that clung to my neck and waist when I held him.

When we were on our trip, we had our mail sent to us. One of the pieces of mail was from the transplant agency. "Mr. and

Mrs. Bates, thank you for your donation. Your son's eyes are now being used . . . ." I dropped the paper and ran to our room. It's beautiful, but it is heart-wrenching. This should not be.

I knew then, why the family who donated a heart for my friend's daughter didn't want to get in touch with them. It was too hard. It was too painful. I would not want to see the eyes of my son in someone else's face. I don't think that I would want to feel his heartbeat in someone else's chest. The emotional weight of that is heavy. If I think about it too much, I burst into tears.

It's too much.

It is bittersweet knowing that our son lives on in someone else. I am grateful that a person who could not see the color yellow before can see that color now. I am grateful that a person who never saw an orange sunset is able to see it now, and I hope that maybe they love orange sunsets as much as we do and wonder why they appear so beautiful to them. They like them simply because our boy's favorite color was orange, and maybe it is theirs too.

We have had friends tell us, "If one person becomes saved from this, it will be worth it for you, I think." They say it as a comfort, but no. No. No one must be saved from my son's death. A Son has already been given for salvation. He was wounded. He was broken, and he was scarred. God didn't need my son to save someone, because he had already given his.

I don't have answers for the why. My heart and brain hurt too much to muse on that any longer. All I know is that my Lord is sovereign, and he died for just this. He died for this death, and he conquered it. My boy may be broken. I may be broken, but my Lord was far more broken for a much higher price than either my son or me.

I think that people compare us to Abraham's sacrifice of his son, Isaac, when God told him to go to Mt. Moriah and make the sacrifice. I get it, I guess, but Abraham never sacrificed his son. God provided a ram in the thicket. Abraham never had to sacrifice his son. I didn't have to sacrifice my children for someone to get to know Jesus. I didn't have to suffer that pain for someone else; Jesus already did. Our suffering can be because we simply live in a very, very broken and sinful world, and pain is a part of living.

Even in these musings, I am not sure why God chose us to walk the road that we have had to walk. I don't know why, but I do know that my Lord is sovereign, and I trust him even when it is beyond hard.

Chapter 10
Humpty Dumpty Back Together Again?

I lay down and slept; I woke again, for the LORD sustained me.

—Psalm 3:5

So we do not lose heart. Though our outer self is wasting away, our inner self is being renewed day by day. For this light momentary affliction is preparing for us an eternal weight of glory beyond all comparison, as we look not to the things that are seen but to the things that are unseen. For the things that are seen are transient, but the things that are unseen are eternal.

—2 Corinthians 4:16–18

No parent ever thinks about the songs they will sing or the verse they will quote during their son's memorial service. But we have. Twice. We put 2 Corinthians 4:16–18 on the program for Boston's service, and we sang "Solid Rock" and "It Is Well with My Soul" just like we did at Eli's service. It seems that the weekend before Eli's birthday or Boston's birthday or the day that Boston went Home, one of these songs was sung in church. We are reminded that God remembers, but I cry through the whole thing.

The Sunday before Boston's fifth birthday, they played *It Is Well with My Soul* in church. I ugly cried through the whole thing. I cried because I missed my son, but I also cried because of the truth in the song. *"Whatever my lot, thou has taught me to say, it is well. It is well with my soul."* I may be able to say, "It is well with my soul," but only through tears of grief and begging God for grace for the next minute. And in all honesty, we barely made it through his fifth birthday. God's grace was evident.

It has now been three years since The Accident. I am the mother of six children. (I had a very early miscarriage between Ellison and Boston. It was during my sister's wedding. Mike and I knew that we would lose the baby before we left Seattle. We decided to keep it under wraps during all the festivities. At the end of each day, we would go to our room and weep together.) Three are at Home before me. Three are still here, and we now have children who are walking through grief along with us, and there have been a lot of times when it has been ugly. Tempers can get short. Grief and sorrow can take us unexpectedly in a moment when we are reminded of monster trucks, big blue eyes, funny comments about bacon, awkward moments, and other Boston-isms that only our family and close friends know.

We try to compartmentalize stuff so we can make it through the day, but sometimes, it is simply impossible, and we have to face our pain and fear head on.

We are homeschoolers, and our kids do online schooling for a few classes. They get to sit and chat with classmates, watch their teacher via video, participate in an online discussion with their peers, read books, and submit projects. It's been a great experience for the kids and for us. They really love the interaction, and we've even had opportunities for our children to meet their teachers in our travels.

Our daughter, Ellison, took a literature class last year and one of the books she read was *Dangerous Journey* (a version of John

Bunyan's *Pilgrim's Progress)*. One of the questions for the discussion that week asked what the kids were most afraid of and why. As part of the assignment, they discussed how they had overcome—or if they were in the process of overcoming—a particular fear. Their teacher gave an example of her fear of spiders. At the time, they were going through the chapter of the book when Christian had to walk through a cave. He was fighting the dragon and Psalm 23 was quoted in the story, *"Even though I walk through the valley of the shadow of death, I will fear no evil, for you are with me; your rod and your staff, they comfort me"* (Ps. 23:4).

When Ellison saw the question, she said, "I'm not answering this. Nope." And quickly walked away. I knew why she didn't want to answer it, and neither did I. I didn't want to take the time to sit with her and unpack it. I didn't want to go there, not because I didn't want to go there with her, but I didn't want to go there myself.

Ellison's fear is real. Her fear also isn't bad. I have the same fears and so do the other members of our family. We're afraid of another family member dying. We're afraid of something tragic and bad happening again. It is easy for us to hop on the "fear bus" and let it overtake us.

Ellison also didn't want to be so transparent with her new friends and teacher in class. She didn't want to share her fear because she also knew that it was a lot bigger than being afraid of the dark or of spiders. She knew that her fear was real, and she also knew that she hadn't, and probably wouldn't, overcome it.

I emailed her teacher and talked with her about The Accident and our true fears. I told her that Ellison would answer the question, but it may not be publicly. I knew that Ellison and I (and all of us) had to take the time to unpack the question together. To sit and talk about our fears and acknowledge that it's okay to be afraid. We would have to talk about our constant struggle with anxiety that something bad could come to pass again. When our worst nightmares and fears come to pass, it's difficult to not be afraid of something happening again. I also don't believe it's sinful for us to be afraid of something bad happening, though we do sin when we choose to camp out and succumb to worry. But even still, grace abounds.

We ended up having Ellison write an answer to the question. Her teacher gave her an option of sending it to her privately or putting it up on the message board. After talking about it, we gave her that option as well. We wanted her to write her answer because in life, we need to do the scary things we don't always want to. We also need to do things that cause us to be vulnerable. She decided that she wanted to share her answer with her friends. She said:

> I have a fear of something bad happening to the people I love. A couple of years ago, our family had a bad accident, and it was really scary, and it was very hard for our family. Jesus has helped us a lot. We've had a lot of visits from Grandma and Grandpa, and we've visited a lot of friends. I ask Jesus to help me not to be afraid like he helped Christian in the book.

She didn't want to talk about details, and that was okay. It was hard enough to say what she did.

Jesus knew that we would be fearful. He knew that we would struggle. He knew that bad things were going to happen. He came as one of us, so he could feel our emotions, our fears, our struggles and pain. He was never naïve about it. When he is telling us not to be afraid, it isn't a command. It's more of a reminder—a reminder that he is present. A reminder that he is near. A reminder that he is the God of peace. A reminder of who he is and why he came to die in our place. He conquered fear on the cross, but he is also aware that we live in a sinful world. Fear will be our constant struggle because the world is a scary place without hope. "*Fear not, little flock, for it is your Father's good pleasure to give you the kingdom*" (Luke 12:32).

Ellison understands this. She understands that this is a constant struggle and that Jesus is the only true Comforter. We have a list of verses that we read when we are afraid. We read Psalms. We read the Bible, whatever it falls open to. We read *The Jesus Storybook Bible*, and sometime, we just cry and get mad and struggle. Praying constantly for Jesus to help us. Grief doesn't disappear. Ever.

The summer after The Accident, I needed Jesus. Badly. (I still do.) It seemed that he had left. He hadn't, but it felt like it. I got an email from She Reads Truth about a Bible study called, "Mourning to Dancing," a 14-day study of laments in the Bible. They took the topics of grief and joy and wrote out scriptures to go with each topic. Then, we had to write a lament in response to the scriptures that we had read. I thought that was right up my alley, and it would give me something to focus on.

Remember my friend Jackie in Seattle? Her son, Zeke, went Home at four months because of SIDS a few years prior. She and her husband, Sam, had become dear friends over the years, so I called her and asked if she wanted to do the grief study with me. She agreed. My kids were in VBS for a week. Every morning that week, I went to the park, read the Bible and cried. I didn't read any commentary, just the Bible. My responses and laments were groanings. I repeated myself each day. Asking God why. Asking God to heal my heart. Asking God to make it all go away. My lament was certainly no amazing Davidic Psalm.

One thing I learned while I studied was that the Psalmists and the Prophets were real! They were honest with their feelings when it came to their difficult circumstances. They groaned and cried with deep yearnings for their Lord to save them. They cried for their people. They were afraid, and they weren't afraid for God to know. In fact, they *wanted* him to! But in those yearnings and groanings, they always spoke of God's everlasting, steadfast love. His never-ceasing love. His *hesed* love. A love so amazing that we can't describe it with an English word because it is too vast.

The prophets were honest, and they cried out to God. They continued to come back to the Truth of God's great compassion for them. They **knew** they had hope even before Hope came to earth. They were secure in his steadfastness. With that, I knew that it was okay to yell and scream and holler, to question, and even to let out a bucket full of swear words as long as I always came back and acknowledged my Savior's love for me. He is not absent. I am not hopeless, and I believe I can say along with the Psalmist, with some confidence (depending on the day), "*You make known to me the path of life; in your presence there is fullness of joy; at your right hand are pleasures forevermore*" (Ps. 16:11).

Jackie and I spoke on the phone that summer, and we talked in person later in the fall when we made a trip to Seattle. One evening, we were sitting with Jackie and her husband, Sam, around the firepit in their backyard. We had all lost children, and we spent the night talking deeply. At one point, Jackie said, "The gospel is enough. We are going to walk through pain and suffering until we are Home. In our suffering, we can praise our Lord through tears for the advancement of the gospel, and he will see us through." I was struck by her grace, and I know that it is a daily reminder for both of us. We need the gospel just as much as the next person.

While I was on bedrest with Eli, a friend had brought over a book called *Stepping Heavenward* by Mrs. Elizabeth Prentiss. I didn't have much of a taste for it at first. But I decided to pick it up one day. I started the book over again and, with each turning of the page, I learned something new. I read the journey of Katy's life. She had lost her father, got married, struggled with illness, struggled in marriage, struggled with relationships, and lost a child, and she relished in the wisdom of others who had gone before her. As she matured throughout the book, I learned something real and true about God's grace and mercy for daily living on each page. I learned about God's goodness in the pages of that book and how he sacrificed his whole life, not just the cross, but the life that he lived out on earth. It was full of suffering. He understands my pain; prior to my personal Sunday School, I didn't believe he or anyone else did.

Mrs. Campbell became my favorite character in the book. While she was sick, she couldn't move. She had already lost her husband and children but continued to encourage and love on Katy. She said:

> Before I go, I want once more to tell you how good He is, how blessed it is to suffer with Him, how infinitely happy He has made me in the very hottest heat of the furnace. It will strengthen you in your trials to recall this my dying testimony. There is no wilderness so dreary but that His love illuminates it, no desolation so desolate but that He can sweeten it. I know what I am saying. It is no delusion. I believe that the highest, purest happiness is known only to those who have learned Christ in sickrooms, in poverty, in racking suspense, and anxiety. . . . To learn Christ, this is life![2]

I have learned "Christ in sickrooms, in poverty, in racking suspense, and anxiety," and I have learned Christ at the open grave. I've learned Christ through lost expectations. I have learned Christ through suffering as many have. Am I blessed to suffer? Yes, I think so. I know so, but I only now know that I am blessed to suffer because of the grace of the gospel although I still struggle with it. Even after The Accident, I can say that I am blessed to struggle,

---

[2] Elizabeth Prentiss, *Stepping Heavenward* (Elgin, IL: David C. Cook Publishing Company, 1901), 88.

but I do it through clenched teeth and many times with an anxious heart. Sometimes with a peaceful heart. I need the true story every day. I need the gospel. I need to be reminded that I can be content in suffering, even in a world that takes pity on the suffering and strife.

I started reading *Stepping Heavenward* for a third (or maybe sixth) time, but when I got to the part where Katy loses her son, I slammed the book shut in frustration, and I haven't picked it up again.

Last summer, we were listening to someone give a testimony at church. The couple was up on stage sharing about how their son had what they thought to be an ear infection that turned into a scary virus. His condition quickly became life threatening, and he was taken to Children's Hospital in Kansas City. The doctors were able to stabilize him, and he went home and healed but needed therapy for quite some time. The point of the story was to show God's faithfulness in prayer and how God had healed their son. In their testimony, they made a comment about God saving their son because people had prayed. I got up, walked out of the church, and found an alcove in the building. I bent over and cried and moaned to Jesus. We prayed. Why didn't he save our sons? I stood there crying, moaning, and questioning without any answers.

Mike came and found me standing there, and we cried together. We had no answers, just empty hands and broken hearts. Soon after, two new friends, Jeremy and Kim, came looking for us. They had seen us leave. They knew that our hearts hurt. They were broken for us, and they didn't have words nor understanding, but they have Jesus, and they had willing shoulders for us to shed our tears. This was huge for me. People stepped into our pain. They even pushed their way in a little bit. They came looking for us, and they were Jesus's hands and feet in a moment of grief for us, and they walked in and comforted us by being present.

Not every child is healed. Not every child makes it through a virus. Not all babies are born healthy. Some are taken far too quickly in the early months from SIDS. Accidents happen, and pain is deep and, in the midst of it all, our Savior is near to the broken parents who got a devastating diagnosis and whose children are fighting for their lives. He is also near to the parents who have had little ones and big ones go Home too soon. Jesus is faithful in it all.

Our pain may be deep, but it is no deeper than the pain of one who has been wounded by the church or has lost a job they held for 20+ years. Jesus is faithful in it all.

Our pain may be deep, but it is no deeper than the pain of one who is suffering from cancer or going through a horrible divorce. Jesus is faithful in it all.

Our pain may be deep, but it is no deeper than the pain of one who loses a spouse or a child who is born with disabilities. The gospel will advance no matter our suffering. Jesus is faithful in it all.

Our pain is deep, and it cannot be compared to our neighbor's because their pain is deep for them, and it must be recognized as such. We can compare pain, but it does no good and only births pride. Instead, we must serve and love and listen because life is difficult and bearing one another's burdens does not look like comparing one another's burdens.

The words of 2 Corinthians 4:16–18 have been a balm to the soul. We put these verses on the cover of the program for Eli's and Boston's services, and I would continually go back to them over the years. I have these verses memorized, but I still read them and murmur them under my breath. I have rocked back and forth on my bed chanting, "light momentary affliction. Preparing for us an eternal weight of glory," not believing the words that I have been saying but still saying them in hopes that they would penetrate my heart in some way. Grasping for truth. Believe in the unseen. Believe in the hope that Jesus gives. Believe that he died for this. Believe that this isn't all there is. Because if this is it, what's the point? None of this seems light or momentary, except as viewed through the lens of eternity.

I had a conversation with someone on Facebook not too long ago about these verses. She said that she didn't think she could believe them, that our life has not looked like "light momentary affliction." I agreed with her, and I told her that if I was honest in my response to these verses, I would say that I have been angry. I have yelled at God; I have told him that he had to show up or I would be done. It has been an ugly, real, and raw grief. But God? He has proven faithful, not just to me, but to so many people who have struggled and have tried to cling or simply been dragged in their faith through deep guttural suffering.

I believe that when we are suffering, we want to make it about ourselves. We want God to fix what is happening. Bring our children back. Put our marriages back together. Make our children normal. Give us a job. Relieve us from financial struggle. The things we suffer on this earth are endless. We are not free of suffering. Not until we get Home.

We demand of God that he take our suffering. We can go and "lay it at the cross" for a few moments of peace, but Jesus already took our suffering. He already bore it. He already died for it. However, we live in the already and the not yet. Jesus already took our suffering, and he already conquered death, but he has not come back to take us to the new heaven and the new earth, which he is creating. We are still struggling with the sin and brokenness of this earth. It is the tension in which we live. It is not going to get better until we are Home, but at the same time, we can live in the hope that "It is finished." God's goodness and glory lie in the finished work of his Son.

I do not want people to pity me. I am apt to pity anyone who has suffered a great deal. I used to pity myself, and I used to want someone to pity me. I *wanted* their pity because then it would appear that I was worse off than they were. Then, I would want them to know everything I had been through to make them feel bad because their suffering seemed trite in comparison. That's straight up pride. That's pride in my pain, and that's sinful.

Instead, I want them to see Jesus. I want them to see his goodness in how he has been enough. How Jesus has been sufficient when we have lost things and people that we held dear. I want them to see that Jesus is more than me. I want them to see that somehow Jesus saw us as worthy to go through the fire again and again. Yes, he is in the fire with us, but I believe that those words sound trite to the suffering.

Our society has a hard time suffering. We are horrible sufferers simply because we are in a "we work hard, we get it" society. We are good, and good comes to us. We do something kind. Good things happen to us. We live in the land of belief in karma, even within the church—that if we obey the rules, things will turn out well.

I thought that. I thought, "I went on mission trips. I went to church. I was a good kid. My marriage was good. I kept going to church every Sunday. I was good! Why was all of this stuff happening?"

Suffering isn't about our goodness. Suffering isn't a repercussion of the bad things that we have done. Yes, Jesus disciplines those he loves because there are consequences for our actions, but when my daughter was born with Down syndrome and our boys were taken Home before us, it wasn't because of anything that we did. It wasn't for our sin. Like when Jesus spoke to his disciples about the blind man before he healed him when they asked what his parents did to make him blind. His parents didn't do anything to cause their son to be blind; they simply lived in a broken world and needed Jesus to save them. It's the same thing. We didn't do anything to bring suffering upon ourselves; we simply live in a broken and sinful world. We live in a place that needs Jesus, and we need Jesus in the midst of our brokenness.

> *"In the world you will have tribulation. But take heart; I have overcome the world."*
>
> —John 16:33

For many years, I believed that my identity was simply a grieving person. I felt like Job while he spoke with his friends. Friends gave advice. I would sometimes listen. I would groan and wonder why God was doing what he was doing, and I wanted answers, but it didn't mean that I was going to get them. I didn't like my identity because I figured that I had a scarlet letter, identifying me as someone who was broken and didn't have her act together. I was that mom. The grieving one. The one with the disabled kid. The one who had needed help for far too long. The one who continued to suffer, even after it seemed the suffering should be done.

Then, I started reading Ephesians 1 and 2. I read them over and over. I still do. I need to be reminded that:

- I have been blessed with every spiritual blessing (v. 3)
- He chose me before the foundation of the world to be holy and blameless (v. 4)
- In love, he adopted me (v. 5)
- He blessed me in the Beloved (v. 6)
- I have redemption through his blood. Forgiveness of sins (v. 7)
- I have been lavished with grace (v. 8)

- He made known to me the mystery of his will through his Son (v. 9)
- I've obtained an inheritance according to his will (v. 11)
- I have hope in Christ (v. 12)
- The gospel is our salvation and we are sealed with the promise of the Spirit (v. 13)

And that's just in the first chapter.

I am his. Forever I am his. I am forever in his grip. It doesn't matter how much my heart hurts. How much the world around me explodes. How my relationships break. How much I mess up. I am his forever. This is true of all of us who believe. We are forever his:

> *For I am sure that neither death nor life, nor angels nor rulers, nor things present nor things to come, nor powers, nor height nor depth, nor anything else in all creation, will be able to separate us from the love of God in Christ Jesus our Lord.*
>
> —Romans 8:38–39

A regular greeting when we see people is, "Hey, how ya doing?" and a typical response is, "Good!" After The Accident, I stopped responding with, "Good!" I wasn't "good," and I wasn't going to pretend I was. So now when I'm asked how I'm doing, I respond with, "I'm okay," "Hanging in there," or (my personal favorite) "I woke up." People would chuckle at the last response, probably because it sounds funny, but the truth of the matter is, I woke up. I got out of bed and faced another day walking in grief, and Jesus was gracious enough to have me wake up and walk me through the day, even if I wasn't paying attention.

Psalm 3:5 says, *"I lay down and slept; I woke again, for the Lord sustained me."*

I realized the other day, that sleeping and waking when we are suffering is simply an evidence of God's grace. Every day, waking is God's grace, and sleeping a full night without nightmares is God's grace. God's grace is evident in the things we simply cannot do on our own. He is present, and he sustains us.

Afterword
For Our Good?

And we know that for those who love God all things work together for good, for those who are called according to his purpose.

—Romans 8:28

We got a great house dog named Lucy last October. My youngest daughter grew to love the dog dearly and took care of her. Lucy followed her everywhere, slept on her bedroom floor, and whined when the kids were outside. We all grew to love Lucy.

We live near the intersection of two busy highways, and Ellison would get nervous, thinking that the dog might be hit by a car. She would open the door every 10 minutes or so and call Lucy to come back into the house where it's safe. We have gotten frustrated with our daughter because she needed to know where the dog was at all times, but we also knew that the dog needed some freedom to roam and be a dog.

I would tell my daughter, "Don't worry. She'll be fine. She'll be back." My daughter would look at me angrily and say, "You can't guarantee that!" She's right. I can't.

I love Romans 8. It is one of my favorite chapters in the Bible. It is full of rich truth. In the beginning of the chapter when Apostle Paul is talking about who we are and what Jesus has done, I get a charismatic excitement in my gut. I love it.

If you were to open my Bible to Romans 8, you would notice that its pages are highlighted, circled, underlined, and have many notes in the margins. It is a favorite. I have a friend who says, "Romans 8 is my jam." It is becoming my jam, too. Between Romans 8 and Ephesians 1, I feel like these passages can refresh my soul in each rereading.

However, there is a section of Romans 8 that often gets pulled out of context in some Christian circles. When I'm reminded of this out-of-context reading, I will sit, reread and struggle through Romans 8 again. We Christians often use Romans 8:28 like inspirational Dayspring cards for the bereaved in hopes of bringing comfort. Instead, Romans 8:28 becomes a mere band-aid for the hurting soul.

Christians often want to jump directly to Romans 8:28 for comfort. But consider the overall context. Throughout the book of Romans, Paul is making his case for the gospel, and when he gets to Romans 8, he spends most of his focus telling us that life is going to be hard and arduous. He talks about suffering (v. 18), future glory (vv. 18–25), and in verses 24 and 25, he says, "*Now hope that is seen* ***is not hope.*** *For who hopes for what he sees?* ***But if we hope for what we do not see, we wait for it with patience***" (emphasis mine).

God's grace is evident in the hard and the pain. It is not only evident in what we see. The stuff that we have, the physical miracles that take place in our health and provision are not the only evidences of grace throughout our life. Paul reminds us not to hope for what we see, but rather to hope for what we do not see. Home. Jesus. Eternity with him.

Each breath we breathe is evidence of God's grace. Each morning we wake up is evidence of God's grace. Each evening we rest our head on the pillow is evidence of God's grace. He is for us. He is with us. He is in our suffering, and he is gracious.

Our family had gotten into a pretty good groove with Lucy, but a couple of weeks ago, on a bright beautiful day, our dog was hit by a car. We were all devastated. It brought back a lot of memories for us. We got through the rest of the day with lots of tears and hugs, but my daughter was right; I can't guarantee anything. I can't guarantee their safety or the dog's.

If I told my daughter right now, "Don't worry, all things work out for our good," she would be horrified and insulted. Her pain isn't just about the death of a dog—which is very sad—but it brought back a lot of memories for her and for the rest of us.

The "all things work together for good" that Paul mentions, is a good found in Christ. When we are in Christ, we are good *despite* our earthly comforts not because of our circumstances. The good that Paul talks about doesn't mean feeling good or being happy all the time. The good means that we are secure. We are loved. We are held. In Christ, there is hope, joy, and peace. God's purpose is for us to belong to him. Romans 8:28 is like a warm blanket to the soul, but we are less likely to experience that warm blanket until we have a fuller understanding of the passage.

- Verse 26: The Spirit helps us in our weakness. When we can't pray, the Spirit intercedes for us.
- Verse 27: He knows us. The Spirit searches our hearts to know what to pray for.
- Verse 29: God chose us to be like Christ.
- Verse 30: God chose, justified, and glorified us because we are in Christ, and we are his children, just as Jesus is his Son.

In the last section of Romans 8 (verses 31–39), Paul gives a beautiful picture of God's love for us through his Son.

What then shall we say to these things? If God is for us, who can be against us? He who did not spare his own Son but gave him up for us all, how will he not also with him graciously give us all things? Who

> *shall bring any charge against God's elect? It is God who justifies. Who is to condemn? Christ Jesus is the one who died—more than that, who was raised—who is at the right hand of God, who indeed is interceding for us. Who shall separate us from the love of Christ? Shall tribulation, or distress, or persecution, or famine, or nakedness, or danger, or sword? As it is written,*
>
> > *"For your sake we are being killed all the day long;*
> > *we are regarded as sheep to be slaughtered."*
>
> ***No, in all these things*** *we are more than conquerors through him who loved us. For I am sure that neither death nor life, nor angels nor rulers, nor things present nor things to come, nor powers, nor height nor depth, nor anything else in all creation, will be able to separate us from the love of God in Christ Jesus our Lord* (emphasis mine).

In ALL things. That means in tribulation, in distress, in suffering, in persecution, in death, and in life. We are conquerors because he loves us, not so that we can avoid pain and suffering. In these verses, there is contentment, life everlasting, lavishing grace, and super-glued love.

I believe and understand now that, when God works all things together for our good, he already has because he has died for us; he has conquered sin and death, and he has given us new life. It is not because God will use our circumstances for something amazing, but rather because of his purpose for us, being his children. He has already worked it for our good through his Son Jesus. That, right there, is in and of itself an evidence of God's grace. God knew that we would need a Rescuer, so he sent his Son. We need him to make it through to the morning. He sustains us. He lavishes us with his grace in the midst of our darkest and brightest days. His grace is in constant abundance.

When I sat in church listening to those evidences of God's grace, I was frustrated at how trite the shout-outs were, but only because of pride in my own pain. I knew people were grateful to God for good things; however over time, I have learned that grace is most evident in our pain and suffering.

After Lucy passed away, the kids didn't want to see her body. Mike and I took care of her and buried her. Later, the kids asked where we had placed her. In time, they all went to the freshly dug grave and over the next several days, my children grieved. I believe that ability to grieve was a gift of grace.

We have pictures of Boston all over the house, and we reminisce about him often—about the funny things he did. Some days are hard, but we don't always enter into grief. We still must live life and accomplish things. Grief can be crippling if we let it.

When the kids went to visit Lucy's grave, they were able to grieve her loss, but not only Lucy's. They're learning to grieve their brother's loss, too. Grief may be crippling, but it is also a healing, grace-filled emotion. Our Lord grieves our sin and aches for us. Jesus grieved his friend Lazarus. He grieved in the Garden. Our Father grieved his Son when he died for us. There is no greater grace than the grace shown to us by our Savior who knows our pain and suffering.

Even now, with the depth of pain that our family has been dealt, I am grateful for a Savior who is with us and grieves with us. I cannot ask for more.

Acknowledgments

This book wouldn't have made it into publishing without some very special people. I appreciate them more than they know, not just because of their contribution but because they have been my cheerleaders along the way, and I couldn't have done it without their encouragement.

Karen and Robert Hicks, Mom, and Dad, you have been on the front lines. Thank you. Along with Amanda Bellisario, my sister, you have prayed, played with my children, and cleaned my microwave far more times than I can count. Angie and Jess Hopson, Jackie and Craig Marais, and Jon and Katie Krombein, you guys have been on the front lines as well, but you have also been neck-deep in our grief more than once. Thank you. Our family loves you guys very much and appreciates you more than words can say. Liz and Ian Huff, you have walked with us, made us meals, shared many conversations over wine and sushi, and we love that we get to walk this life with you. Sam and Jackie Jarawan, your back deck is one of my favorite spots. Jesus has met us there countless times as we bore one another's burdens. Dick and Tami McKinley, you have loved us well, and you are some of our dearest friends. Jason and Kristina Wendorf, you are dear friends, and we appreciate your honesty and love for us. Mandy Haverly, Kevin and Ginger Presley, Ben and Amanda Hammon, and Stephanie Nelson, we met and connected through life's happenings, and we are grateful for knowing you, even if it was through our sufferings. Gary and Sarah Burns, John and Missi Wilson, Angela Giboney, Josh and Lexi Clayton, Addie Gerlach, Mike and Rebecca Vierra, Kathy Giotta, Kelly Bouchard, Matt and Leah Boutell, Pete and Debbie VanDuyne, thank you for being our cheerleaders, for urging us on and praying for us. We are grateful for you in our lives. Auntie Di, Uncle Tim, Aunt Mary, Aunt Vicki, and John, thank you for your prayers and support. Kelsey Keizer, Connie Pruitt, and Jessica Ghioni, you guys helped make this happen. Thank you.

I could list so many names of people to thank for their friendship, listening ears, and sacrificial hearts and for the many hours invested in my family and me. You know who you are. Thank you. Thank you for being my cheerleaders and for your encouragement and love through the years. I truly could not have overcome without your many "atta girls!" whispered in my ear.

CPSIA information can be obtained
at www.ICGtesting.com
Printed in the USA
FSHW021330211119

9 781632 963574